A FORK IN THE ROAD

CHOOSE **POVERTY** OR **PROSPERITY**

A PRACTICAL GUIDE TO WINNING AT LIFE

VIDAR LIGARD

SAFARI
MISSION

Tulsa, OK

A Fork in the Road
Copyright © 2020 by Vidar Ligard.

Library of Congress Control Number: 2020938766
ISBN: 978-1-7348655-0-9 (US Paperback). Printed in the United States of America.

Published by Safari Mission.
Tulsa, Oklahoma, USA.
www.safarimission.org

A huge thank you to

My wife, Cathrine
you always encourage me to climb higher

My parents
you gave me a solid foundation in life

The Hagin family
you taught me to walk with God and propelled my life to new levels

The faculty at Oral Roberts University
you trained me to make no little plans

My many, many friends and mentors
you coached, inspired, and helped shape me

Contents

Preface

I magine people who have grown up in unfortunate circumstances, seemingly without opportunities, and not having much hope in life. It is marvelous to see them start to understand the principles of growth and success, start applying them, and then come out of those circumstances that seemed hopeless.

Many have dreams and will often spend years wishing for them to come to pass, but as time goes on, the hope of those dreams often fade. It is amazing to see such people start to understand the principles that make dreams come to pass and start moving visions from the realm of hope into reality.

Over the years, my wife, Cathrine, and I have seen countless stories of those who have started understanding the principles of success, growth, and building the future. When those principles are believed and action is taken, the future of personal lives, businesses, churches, schools, and entire communities can be dreamed, planned, designed, and purposefully built.

Cathrine and I have lived, worked, traveled, and ministered on three continents. The challenges that face humanity are the same everywhere. There are people all over the globe who wish they were in a different position in life. People want their circumstances, surroundings, and life situations to be better. The answers to humanity's problems are the same everywhere. We have spent the last decade and a half teaching principles that help people come out of poverty, make dreams come true, and form circumstances that make a different future both for themselves and those around them.

God told Joshua that if he would think, speak, and act according to God's Word, he would be successful (Joshua 1:8). Jesus told us that if we would hear His Word and act upon it, we would be able to stand the storms of life (Matthew 7:24–25). Solomon was the richest man there was, and he wrote a book—the book of Proverbs—filled with the principles of success.

The fork in the road is a choice. My desire is for your future to be better, so I am sharing the principles I have found to work with you. Choose the high road.

God bless you.

Vida

Vidar

CHAPTER 1

Start With Yourself

Our Journey

In 2014 Cathrine and I were stuck, and I was extremely frustrated. We had pioneered four Bible college campuses in Kenya. In the eyes of many, we had stepped out and accomplished something. My wife and I no longer lived the typical life, working 8 a.m.–5 p.m. Monday through Friday. We'd founded missions work in East Africa and overcome lots of challenges to get to that point. But we were stuck. Over a period of years, the school wasn't growing past 70 students. We had lots of passion, drive, and vision to see a much larger work, but year after year, student enrollment remained the same.

My wife and I were well educated. Between us, we had degrees in engineering, church administration, and business administration, in addition to years of Bible and practical ministry studies. We applied ourselves during our school years, and both graduated with glowing reviews. But even with all of those degrees and credentials, we were stuck.

Not only were we educated, but we worked hard as well. I kept a stressful job as an IT director for Kenneth Hagin Ministries in Oklahoma, overseeing nine employees. When I got home, ate dinner, and put our young girls to bed, I would work on our Bible colleges in Kenya often until midnight, and sometimes until 2 a.m. These were years with long hours of hard work, but we were passionate and glad to do it. Still, with the benefits of our education and hard work, we weren't satisfied with where we were.

I remember looking at some Bible schools in other nations that were doing better than our schools in Kenya. I'd think about running those schools instead of the ones we started. After all of the time and effort we'd poured into our schools, it felt unfair that we weren't doing better. I was frustrated and tempted to leave it all and go somewhere else. The grass looked greener on the other side. Those schools were thriving in better environments. They had better team members and things were growing. Like most everyone, I wanted to be part of something that was growing. I had a hint of envy toward the people who got to run those "better schools," and I thought those must be easier schools to manage.

Similarly, everywhere I go, I find people who are dreaming of being in a better situation. People often want to be on a level higher than where they are. As I was thinking of one of these other schools, I fancied myself in the position of their director or general manager. Then I started asking myself what decisions and direction I would take in order to grow that school further. I quickly found out that I didn't quite know what to do to grow this particular school. So I realized it probably wasn't such a great idea to run an organization if I didn't know what to do to bring it further. Then I started thinking of another school that was in a similar situation as we were, but thriving and growing. I thought, "Surely, I could run that one." But as I envisioned myself taking the helm, I knew again that I could not set out a five-year plan for that school either.

A bit disappointed and dissatisfied, I thought of the schools we had in Kenya and wondered what would happen to them if one of the

4

directors of these thriving schools came to run our schools. It didn't take long to realize that the directors of those schools would come to Kenya, make some changes, and the schools would start to grow.

For quite some time, I had looked at circumstances and external factors, trying to figure out why our schools weren't growing. But when I compared our schools to others, and thought about other directors and myself switching positions, I realized each of the schools were at the level they were because of what the leaders brought to the table.

I finally found the problem even though it was a painful, humbling realization. The reason we were stuck was found in my bathroom mirror every single morning staring back at me. We were stuck because we had grown the school to the level of my own leadership capacity.

> WE WERE STUCK BECAUSE WE HAD GROWN TO THE LEVEL OF MY OWN LEADERSHIP CAPACITY.

Any of the other directors would make changes in Kenya, and things would start growing. And if I was placed at one of their schools, I wouldn't quite know what to do and we would be in maintenance mode. I was well aware that any organization only trying to hold on to its current position would shrink.

Realizing I was the problem was a huge challenge, but also very liberating. At least the problem was one I had control over. It is much better to have a problem or challenge I can control, than to try to blame some external variable I can't control.

So, I set a goal of developing myself personally. For one entire year, I set all other goals aside. I didn't care about trying to grow our schools. I knew I was the one that had to change and grow. Once that was done, growing our schools would be easy.

Only a few months later, we were at a ministers retreat, and everyone was sharing what their goals were for the year. Everyone had goals of growing their church, adding something to their buildings, or starting a better children's program. Many were surprised when they heard my goal was simply personal development. That was several years ago now, and I have noticed that we have grown a lot in our organization, and many of those ministers have not grown very much at all.

Today, we have nine campuses in Kenya, have grown to over 250 students, delegated most of our administrative work, and are working on expanding operations into several other nations. Not only that, but our finances have increased about 10 times. It all started with looking in the mirror and deciding that I needed to start with myself.

When I see where others are in life, I find that most everyone wishes they were at a higher level; that they either had more, were accomplishing more, or were more satisfied. Many, while not really satisfied, have settled for where they are in life. They have some excuse for why they are where they are and will usually point to some external circumstance that they don't have control of. Most people are blaming external factors for their lack of progress, but the real problem is found with ourselves, which we *can* control. Most of the time, I don't have to spend much time with people to locate where they are, and it usually doesn't take long to realize why they are not further along than what they are.

To illustrate from the field of ministry: if you take a pastor running a church of 1,000 members and place them over a church of only 100, in almost every case, the small church will start growing. Similarly, if you take a pastor of a 100-member church and place them over a 1,000-member church, it won't be long before the church starts shrinking.

The same is true with money, poverty, and business. If a poor person wins the lottery and becomes a millionaire, it usually won't be long before they have squandered the money and end up in a position worse than they were before they won the money. This happened to one of our neighbors where I grew up in Norway. He placed bets on horse races and one day won big. But he didn't know how to manage all that money, and it wasn't long before he was divorced and lost his house. On the other hand, if you find a self-made millionaire and see them lose everything through a bad business deal, a natural disaster, or a business crook takes advantage of them, it usually won't be long before they find a way of building themselves back up to where they were and grow beyond. Poor people are poor because they have a mindset problem. They don't know how to handle money. Rich people are rich because they have a solid mindset when it comes to finances. We have seen lots of people in Africa come out of poverty by changing their mindset.

There are a number of different areas in our lives we need to master in order to grow ourselves. Once *we* grow, growth in our life and circumstances will follow.

Build the Right Foundation

Currently, I am preparing to climb Mount Kilimanjaro, the highest mountain in Africa at over 19,000 feet (almost 6,000 meters). There are specific preparations I am making. In hiking and mountain climbing, there is a simple quote, "The man on top of the mountain didn't fall there."[1] No one gets to the top by wishing, hoping, or even asking questions. Wishing, hoping, and asking questions are fine, but unless the right sequence of action is taken, I won't find myself at the top of Kilimanjaro. While this mountain is big, virtually anyone and everyone who wants to can reach the summit. It just requires some determination and a willingness to learn a little about the process, then go and do the necessary.

The same is true in life. Having a good, successful, fulfilling, and rewarding life is possible for virtually anyone. And it isn't rocket science. There are principles and actions that, when followed, will build a good life. Many of those principles are found in this book.

But remember, it isn't the person who knows how to climb Kilimanjaro that makes it to the top. It is only those who are determined enough to take consistent action over a period of time.

Anything in life that is worth something of value goes through a process that is deeper than what you see in the finished product. Gold isn't pretty when it first comes out of the mine. The materials in a Rolex watch go through a specific and lengthy process to become something magnificent. Throughout my life, I have met so many people who only focus on positive end results. Those results will never happen without the willingness to go through the process of getting there. Unsuccessful people tend to look at the success of others and wish they had it, but they often do not realize all of the hard work, right choices, and sacrifices it took to get there.

When we think of a wonderful home, we often envision the beautiful finishing touches, exotic wood floor, marble countertops, and the latest fad in wall coverings and ornaments. But all of those finishing touches wouldn't matter unless the foundation is laid correctly, there is quality framing, and the walls and windows are well insulated. These things aren't typically noticed, but are more critical to quality than the last finishing touches.

Finances, success, and satisfaction are the "beautiful finishing touches" in life. All too many focus on money and how to increase income or sell more. Increasing income and sales are not the first place to look. Instead, there are many foundational life attitudes and thought processes that need to be well cemented. And when these are put in place, income and sales become easier, low-hanging fruit.

Wonderful end results are certainly possible and obtainable for anyone. But remember Rome wasn't built in a day. A solid, productive, fulfilling, and successful life is also not created overnight. The good news is the steps to get there are ones that anyone can take and it's a wonderful journey.

IN ORDER TO BUILD A QUALITY LIFE, THERE ARE MANY DIFFERENT AREAS THAT NEED TO BE UNDERSTOOD AND EXECUTED WELL.

The Weakest Link

To build a house correctly, there are many different areas that need to be done properly. The work on the foundation is very different from the electrical work. Putting in the right insulation is very different from installing the wood flooring. But they are all necessary in a quality home. Likewise, in order to build a quality life, there are many different areas that need to be understood and executed well.

A chain is only as strong as its weakest link. When weight is applied, and the weakest link breaks, the chain is no longer good for much of anything. Think about all the systems in a car—the brakes, the drive train, the engine cooling system, the fuel system, the steering, and so on. If one of those systems has a major problem, it will not do any good to add a turbo to the engine to make the car go faster. If the brakes are out, you will have to get them fixed before you can think of making enhancements to systems that are already working. I remember one time my brakes went out on my car, and I had to take it to a nearby mechanic. The mechanic was only a mile away, but that short drive was so nerve-racking. I inched my way there with my hands glued to the steering wheel. It would have been much easier to get there on my bicycle.

Over the years, I have observed that many tend to overemphasize one area of their life while neglecting other important truths. There are many areas that need to be functioning in order for life to be successful. If an accountant is great at their trade but has no people skills, it won't help to improve their technical skills to build a better business. They need to improve their people skills to grow a healthy business.

Over the next several chapters, you will come across underlying thinking processes, various areas that need to be functioning, practical steps to take, and resources for further study and improvement. If you will look to learn, grow, and consistently apply the right principles, you too will make it to the top. The journey takes effort, but the views are enjoyable and the results are marvelous.

Notes
[1] Quote by Vince Lombardi

CHAPTER 2

God Wants You Prosperous

God Is a Good God

God is a good God!

When Oral Roberts started preaching this message in the 1940s and 50s, it was with much opposition. Much of the church world held God responsible for hardships, and therefore were opposed to such a positive message. But Jesus boldly declared, "The thief comes only to steal and kill and destroy. I came that they may have life and have it abundantly" (John 10:10).

When the religious elite complained about Jesus helping sinners and healing the sick, he responded with statements like, "And ought not this woman, a daughter of Abraham whom Satan bound for eighteen years, be loosed from this bond on the Sabbath day?" (Luke 13:16). Or, "I have not come to call the righteous but sinners to repentance" (Luke 5:32). Or, "The Spirit of the Lord is upon me, because he has anointed me to bring good news to the poor . . . . recovery of sight to the blind, . . . to let the oppressed go free. . ." (Luke 4:18–19, NRSV).

Before we can live a good, successful, and prosperous dream life, we must first believe that this is really what God wants for us. He wants us to have life and live it abundantly. Good news isn't only found in the gospels. Throughout Scripture, through every era, we find God giving instructions on how to build and lead a good life—not a self-centered, inward-focused life only looking for personal gain, but a fulfilling life that is full of blessing for both others and us. Consider a few examples from the Old Testament:

- God told Abraham to leave Ur—a large and comfortable city at the time. It was surely a sacrifice to move into an uncivilized, nomadic area and live in tents, but God blessed him and he became very rich in cattle, silver, and gold (Gen. 13:2).

- In the Mosaic covenant, we find great blessings for obedience and following God. We are to be the head and not the tail, blessed going out and coming in, and blessed in the city or in the field. We should be lenders and not borrowers, and the list goes on (Deut. 28).

> GOD IS A GOOD GOD AND HE WANTS HIS PEOPLE BLESSED. TO TRY TO ARGUE THAT HE DOESN'T WANT HIS PEOPLE BLESSED IS EITHER A GROSS IGNORANCE OF SCRIPTURE OR A HYPOCRITICAL ATTACK ON HIS NATURE AS A GOOD FATHER.

- God told Joshua to be careful to follow His instructions and then he would have success everywhere he went (Joshua 1:5–8). Joshua did have success, and Israel grew and expanded under his leadership. Sadly, the next generation would not follow in his footsteps. The book of Judges is known as the book of failure. Other nations kept conquering Israel because the Israelites kept going their own way. Following God leads to a blessed life, but disobeying Him leads to failure.

- David was a man after God's own heart (1 Sam. 13:14, Acts 13:22). While not perfect, he intensely sought to do things God's way. While he was chased from cave to cave by Saul, he still refused to lay hands on Saul when the opportunity came. King Saul went to relieve himself in the very cave where David and his men were hiding. Being a man of character and principle, David refused to lay a hand on the king (1 Sam. 24). Yet, because of his obedience, God exalted him, solidified the throne of David, and led Israel into its greatest season of prosperity.

- Solomon followed in the steps of his father, David, and sought God and His wisdom more than success (2 Chron. 1:10). As a result, Israel became so rich that silver was counted of the same value as rocks (2 Chron. 1:15). Solomon wrote in Proverbs, "Long life is in [wisdom's] right hand; in her left hand are riches and honor" (Prov. 3:16).

- When Israel left God's ways, the kingdom split, and as corruption and immorality increased, the entire nation eventually went into captivity. Even in the midst of the Babylonian captivity, Jeremiah the prophet wrote a letter to the captives with God's instructions, "Build houses and live in them; plant gardens and eat their produce. Take wives and have sons and daughters; take wives for your sons, and give your daughters in marriage, that they may bear sons and daughters; multiply there, and do not decrease" (Jer. 29:5–6).

Babylon was a place of sin and Israel ended up there because of her sin, yet God continued, "But seek the welfare [peace and prosperity] of the city where I have sent you into exile, and pray to the Lord on its behalf, for in its welfare you will find your welfare . . . . For I know the plans I have for you, declares the Lord, plans for wholeness and not for evil, to give you a future and a hope" (Jer. 29:7, 11).

God's mercy and relentless desire to see his people blessed, *even when they had caused their own calamity* is just amazing.

- During captivity, we find people like Daniel, Esther, Nehemiah, and Ezra seeking God, and God again gives His people freedom.

In Haggai, He clearly instructs them to prioritize His house before their own (Hag. 1:4–11). When the people adjusted their priorities, God declared, "But from this day on, I will bless you" (Hag. 2:19).

Every time period in the Old Testament had instructions and examples of prosperity. The instructions are the same in the New Testament:

- "But seek first the kingdom of God and his righteousness, and all these things will be added to you" (Matt. 6:33).

- "... There is no one who has left house or wife or brothers or parents or children, for the sake of the kingdom of God, who will not receive many times more in this time, and in the age to come eternal life" (Luke 18:29–30).

- "... Whatsoever one sows, that will he also reap" (Gal. 6:7).

- "For you know the grace of our Lord Jesus Christ, that though he was rich, yet for your sake he became poor, so that you by his poverty might become rich" (2 Cor. 8:9).

- "The thief comes only to steal and kill and destroy. I came that they may have life and have it abundantly" (the words of Jesus in John 10:10).

- "Every good gift and every perfect gift is from above, coming down from the Father of lights, with whom there is no variation or shadow due to change" (James 1:17).

God is a good God and He wants His people blessed. To try to argue that He doesn't want His people blessed is either a gross ignorance of Scripture or a hypocritical attack on His nature as a good Father.

Prosperity Critics

I have spoken to a number of Christians and ministers who speak against God wanting His people to prosper. One minister I met was quick to mention a few areas of theological disagreement once he found out what church I was affiliated with. He did not like the message that

God wants us to prosper financially. Yet, he was working as a financial advisor during the day and preaching at night. The majority of his on-the-job time was spent helping people to be better off financially. But, at the same time, he believed God didn't want people to prosper. His theology was completely opposed to what he did for a living! How does that make any sense? If he really didn't believe people should be well off financially, he needed to find another career!

Once in Nairobi, my wife and I attended a church service where another missionary preached about how prosperity was wrong. He even went to the point of quoting other ministers, then attacking what they had preached. He was of the opinion that we should be content with what we have and never wish or strive to have more. Nairobi is a metropolitan city of about six million people with huge economic differences between its citizens. It is known both for its slums and its affluence. The interesting part was this particular missionary lived in an area where the very affluent live, and his kids received the best private schooling available in the city. I heard several of the local Nairobians call him out on his hypocrisy.

I also talked to lay people who were against prosperity. I remember one highly educated man lamenting about the message that God wants us to prosper. Yet, only a few moments later, he talked about others who happen to have more than him, and bemoaned how they were better off than him. It was evident in his voice that he wished he was better off financially.

All these are examples of people who want the best, but have the mentality that God doesn't want the best for them. It is sad to watch people who believe God doesn't want them to prosper, but they work their whole life for their own prosperity and well being. That makes it very difficult to live full of peace and joy. Surely, there is great gain in living a content life. (In upcoming chapters, we will discuss attitudes of greed, the love of money, and how selfishness does not lead to a good life.)

There is a very interesting observation with the three examples I mentioned—the minister, the missionary, and the lay person. All of them had taken relatively good care of themselves and their immediate family. To my knowledge, all of them give financially to others. But because of their mindset about prosperity, they don't have much more than just enough for themselves and their family, and they are not in a position to be major blessings to others. The vast majority of their financial well being has gone to themselves and their family.

What we need is churches filled with people who are themselves blessed, generous, and have the means to be major influencers in their societies. When we only barely have enough for ourselves, or are just focused on filling our own storehouse, we are really suffering from being self centered, and it becomes difficult to influence anything outside our own four walls.

> WHAT WE NEED IS CHURCHES FILLED WITH PEOPLE WHO ARE THEMSELVES BLESSED, GENEROUS, AND HAVE THE MEANS TO BE MAJOR INFLUENCERS IN THEIR SOCIETIES.

Remember, God told us what He wants for our lives if we will just do what He's asked of us. "The Lord will open the heavens, His abundant storehouse, to send rain on your land in season and to bless all the work of your hands. You will lend to many nations, but borrow from none. The Lord will make you the head and not the tail; you will only move upward and never downward" (Deut. 28:12–13).

Biblical Role Models

Scriptures and history both have plenty of positive examples of people who walked with God, lived successful lives, and became major blessings to large numbers of people.

King David started his life as a shepherd boy, towards the bottom rung of society in Israel. But because of his dedication to God, he was blessed and lived a life of continual growth. As a young shepherd, he went beyond the call of duty and would kill lions or bears who attacked his father's sheep. Those became experiences he reminded himself of when he needed courage to take out the giant soldier, Goliath, despite his young age. His experience worshiping God brought him before the king as a personal psalmist. But like everyone, he went through challenges in his life, and for a while was hiding in caves. At that time, everyone in debt, in despair, and bitter in soul came to him (1 Sam. 22:2). Yet, David turned the situation around both for himself and those who followed him. Over time, David became king, and his followers became his mighty men. Towards the end of David's life, his men gave 272 tons of gold to the Lord (1 Chr. 29:4, 7). In today's value, that would be about $11 billion. David followed the Lord, the Lord blessed him, and David lived life as a blessing to many.

Solomon, David's son, also followed the Lord and knew he needed wisdom in order to lead people well. When he first became king at a young age, he desired and asked God for the wisdom needed to manage the nation well (1 Kings 3:1–15). Because he put the needs of the nation before his own, the Lord blessed him not only with wisdom, but also with huge amounts of riches and honor. Solomon proceeded to usher in Israel's best period of peace and prosperity to the point that silver became as common as stones (1 Kings 10:27). His actions certainly benefited a whole nation, and royals came from afar just to hear the wisdom of Solomon and see his accomplishments (1 Kings 10:24).

Prosperity isn't limited to God's people in just the Old Testament. In the New Testament, we see some of God's servants with money and influence. At one time, Governor Felix kept calling for Paul while he was in prison, because, "he hoped that money would be given him by Paul" (Acts 24:26). Someone as influential and well off as the governor surely wouldn't keep calling the poorest prisoner, hoping for a bribe. No, corrupt officials of high standing looked for those who seemed to have large means, hoping for bribes. While Paul fell to robbers and was shipwrecked at times, he also knew how to work, handle money, and certainly was a person of much influence. Towards the end of his first imprisonment, he lived in Rome for "two whole years at his own expense, and welcomed all who came to him" (Acts 28:30). With as many as would want to see Paul, I would imagine this to be a larger home, and in the capital of Rome, it almost certainly couldn't have been a cheap shack. But Paul used his wealth to reach a place where he could be a blessing to all who came to him.

Historical Role Models

There are many who think of successful people in terms of them getting ahead at the expense of others. Such thinking is detrimental to your own success. Most people succeed in life by helping and advancing the lives of other people. You should too!

Thomas Edison's most famous invention is the electric light bulb. After studying and experimenting with electricity, he became convinced that there was a way to convert electricity to light. He painstakingly logged over 10,000 experiments trying to create a commercially viable light bulb. Everyone who bought one of those light bulbs decided they would be better off if they parted with a little money and got electric light than if they continued burning candles. Edison made everyone's lives better, and all of us have been happy to part with a little money in order to live a more convenient life. Edison became rich because he helped everyone else get ahead.

MOST PEOPLE SUCCEED IN LIFE BY HELPING AND ADVANCING THE LIVES OF OTHER PEOPLE. YOU SHOULD TOO!

Hans Nielsen Hauge is well known as one of the most influential people in Norwegian history. I grew up going to elementary school in Norway, where we learned about him and how his work made a profound impact both on the church landscape and on industrialization and work ethic in the nation. In the 1700s, Norway was an extremely poor country in Europe. While being the forefront preacher for a spiritual renewal in the country, Hauge would also work to establish businesses, paper mills, newspapers, and salt extraction factories while also teaching people about work ethic, time management, and financial stewardship. His teachings helped usher in both a spiritual revival and an economic renaissance period.

George Müller, a Christian evangelist in England, influenced count-less people, even after his passing. The mainstream of his ministry was caring for orphans in Bristol, England, funding another 9,000 school students, publishing tracts, and providing about 10,000 Bibles annually and supporting 189 missionaries.[2] This, of course, required large amounts of funding and being able to think much larger than the average per-son. He is known for not using any fundraising methods, but simply by praying and trusting God. The unique thing about George Muller is that the orphanage he was most famous for was not his ultimate aim. In is heart was the "desire of setting before the church at large, and before the world, a proof that He [God] has not in the least changed; and this seemed to me best done, by the establishing of an Orphan-House."[3] George Muller wanted to prove that one could take God at His Word and rely on it. His example became a powerful testimony and helped countless others both during and after his lifetime.

A more recent example of a successful, godly family who became a great positive influence is the Green family, the founders of Hobby Lobby. They started out small in 1970[4] and have grown to over $4 bil-lion in revenue with 32,000 employees in over 800 stores.[5] Because of their success, they have a major part in funding Oral Roberts Univer-sity, successfully challenged ungodly government practices before the US Supreme Court,[6] and helped build the Museum of the Bible in Washington, DC. This is in addition to providing work for 32,000 peo-ple so that they can feed their own families. Sure, such success comes with controversy, but their influence and impact cannot be denied.

Notes

[2] George Muller, Answers to Prayer, 2007 edition by Moody Bible Institute. Edited by Rosalie DeRosset, 115–116.

[3] Muller, Answers to Prayer, 23.

[4] Source: https://hobbylobby.com/about-us (accessed June 11, 2019).

[5] Source: https://wikipedia.org/Hobby Lobby (accessed June 11, 2019).

[6] Hobby Lobby proved before the US Supreme Court that private corporations have the right to practice certain religious liberties in the 2014 case of Burwell v. Hobby Lobby.

CHAPTER 3

Create Your Future

Futures Don't Just Happen

Doris Day made a song very popular in the 1950s. The name of the song was "Que Sera, Sera," which means, "Whatever will be, will be." Over the years, I have seen many variations of this attitude; that the events of the future are outside of our control and things are just going to happen anyway. Many seemed to be soothed by the idea that the future is not their responsibility, so why worry or have any cares.

God thinks differently. Life does not just happen. He has given us instructions to follow, and what we do with those instructions will greatly impact our futures.

The story of the nation of Israel going through the wilderness and into the future God desired for them is a good example of this principle. God told Moses and the nation of Israel they would be delivered from Egypt and into the promised land. When they were in the desert, they had seen the hand of God deliver them from Pharaoh through the

Red Sea. They were seeing the pillar of fire at night and the cloud during the day, and they ate supernatural manna daily. Then Moses sent a representative from each of the Israelite tribes to investigate the land they were about to move into. While God had promised to deliver, they did not sit idle and wait for it to happen. They sent spies in order to prepare.

LIFE DOES NOT JUST HAPPEN. HE HAS GIVEN US INSTRUCTIONS TO FOLLOW, AND WHAT WE DO WITH THOSE INSTRUCTIONS WILL GREATLY IMPACT OUR FUTURES.

Ten of the spies came back and reported that the land was impossible to conquer because of the walled cities and the giants. Caleb and Joshua said, "Let us go up at once and occupy it, for we are well able to overcome it" (Num. 13:30). The others looked at the problems, said it could not be done, and brought "an evil report" (Num. 13:32 KJV).

The people had a choice. They could believe Caleb and Joshua, or they could believe the 10 other spies. They chose doubt. Numbers 14:2 shows the extent of their unbelief, saying, "Would that we had died in the land of Egypt! Or would that we had died in this wilderness!" They are saying they would rather have died in Egypt or in the wilderness than even attempt to enter the promised land.

In this story, everyone had an individual choice to make, and they all ended up with a future according to what they chose to believe and the words they spoke. God told them, "As I live, declares the Lord, what you have said in my hearing I will do to you" (Num. 14:28). Everyone 20 years and older ended up dying in the wilderness, except for Joshua and Caleb.

At the end of his life, Caleb talked to Joshua about the secret to how his future was designed, saying, "I was forty years old when Moses the servant of the Lord sent me from Kadesh-barnea to spy out the land, and I brought him word again as it was in my heart" (Joshua 14:7). Instead of speaking according to the difficult circumstances he

22

saw, Caleb spoke from what was in his heart, and he ended up with a different future than everyone else.

Joseph is another example of someone who wouldn't take a laissez-faire approach to his situation. He refused to sit down, quit, and allow circumstances to form his attitude. His emotions must have been a roller coaster as he moved from being ridiculed by his brothers, to almost killed and thrown in a pit (Gen. 37:1–24). I can only imagine the hope he must have felt when he heard a caravan stopping and believed they were rescuing him. Just after he realized that these were his Ishmaelite cousins, they sold him into slavery to Egypt (Gen. 37:25–28). Yet, despite the disappointment, he kept working for Potiphar with such excellence that Joseph was promoted to be in charge of his entire household (Gen. 39:1–4). Those with the attitude that they aren't responsible for any of the circumstances around them never get promotions. If Joseph hadn't controlled his emotions and decided to do excellent work in spite of the fact that it looked like God had let him down, he never would have risen to accomplish what God had in store for him.

But, when it looks like God came through, he was then falsely accused and thrown into prison (Gen. 39:7–20). When life brings a series of such devastating blows, most people I know would cave and give up. Somewhere along the way, it would be easy to become disappointed at family, God, and life in general. It would be easy to dwell on the disappointments and let bitterness set in. But Joseph refused to take the attitude that, "Whatever will be, will be." He held his attitude so high and carried himself with such excellence that it wasn't long before he was in charge of the prison (Gen. 39:21–23). This isn't just a cute story or a fairy tale. God had this recorded for our example. There are lessons here that if we live by, we will come out of desperate situations and walk into the future God has for us.

Sure, Caleb, Joshua, and Joseph didn't create or form every detail of their futures. They each experienced some setbacks along the way. But the point is they had something to do with forming their overall future. Don't stumble over the details; just realize that those who walked with God, even when the circumstances were hard, ended up on top in the end.

The God Way

There is a God way to success. Volumes of books have been written about success, many of them with secular principles, and many of them advocating a success that leads to an empty soul. I have talked to many people, even Christians, who have had great success according to worldly standards, yet experience a lack of satisfaction. God's way to success leads to a healthy and peaceful life. It is a rewarding life full of satisfaction.

During my college years, many of my classmates would greet each other, "How is life treating you?" On the surface, it wasn't much different than asking, "What's new?" But I quickly realized there was an undertone of life being unpredictable. My standard response was, "Life doesn't treat me. I treat life." I was convinced I had more control over circumstances than what most people believed. Of course, we can't predict everything, but by and large, we can design, invent, and create our own futures. In fact, I am utterly convinced that each and every person is supposed to take charge of their future, and make something good of it, not only for themselves, but for those around them. If you don't take charge of your future, someone or something else will.

> IF YOU DON'T TAKE CHARGE OF YOUR FUTURE, SOMEONE OR SOMETHING ELSE WILL.

When Joshua took over the leadership of Israel after Moses died, God gave him the principle for how to take charge of the future.

Joshua 1:5–8

5 No man shall be able to stand before you all the days of your life. Just as I was with Moses, so I will be with you. I will not leave you or forsake you.

6 Be strong and courageous, for you shall cause this people to inherit the land that I swore to their fathers to give them.

7 Only be strong and very courageous, being careful to do according to all the law that Moses my servant commanded you. Do not turn from it to the right hand or to the left, that you may have good success wherever you go.

8 This Book of the Law SHALL NOT DEPART FROM YOUR MOUTH, but you shall MEDITATE ON IT DAY AND NIGHT, so that you may be CAREFUL TO DO ACCORDING TO ALL THAT IS WRITTEN in it. FOR THEN YOU WILL MAKE YOUR WAY PROSPEROUS, AND THEN YOU WILL HAVE GOOD SUCCESS.

Here, God gave instructions for ensuring good success. Some have thought that if we just base our lives on what God said, we will increase our probability of success. But this isn't about probability. *This is an absolute promise of success.* God said, ". . . then you *will* have good success." There *is* a sure way of success and it's actually simple. First, the word of God "shall not depart from your mouth." Second, "you shall meditate on it day and night." Third, "be careful to do according to all that is written in it." That's it! When we think in line with God, speak in line with God, and act accordingly, then our future will be formed in accordance with God's thoughts for us.

In the first Psalm, the writer puts it very similarly.

Psalm 1:1–3

1 Blessed is the man who walks not in the counsel of the wicked, nor stands in the way of sinners, nor sits in the seat of scoffers;

2 but his delight is in the law of the Lord, and on his law he meditates day and night.

3 He is like a tree planted by streams of water that yields its fruit in its season, and its leaf does not wither. IN ALL THAT HE DOES, HE PROSPERS.

It is absolutely possible to be successful. You can choose to live life passively, allowing circumstances to form your life, or you can live above circumstances, ruling and designing them.

Joshua was careful to lead the people according to what God instructed. As a result, at the end of his life he said, ". . . not one word has failed of all the good things that the Lord your God promised concerning you. All have come to pass for you; not one of them has failed" (Joshua 23:14).

Grow Into the Right Mindset

The book of Joshua is known as the book of success. All of God's promises came to pass, and the nation of Israel served God through the next generation as well (Joshua 24:31). The following book, Judges, is known as the book of failure. There is a cycle that kept repeating in Judges. First, during a time of peace and prosperity, the people abandoned the Lord's principles and instructions. Second, their failure to follow God would cause them to fail and eventually be oppressed by the neighboring countries. Third, after a season of oppression, they would call out to the Lord. Fourth, the Lord would answer their prayer, the nation would be delivered through one of the judges, and usher in a new season of peace and prosperity. Then the cycle would start all over again. It is a cycle of human experience that we can find many places in history and also in some of our own individual lives.

When Israel was oppressed by Midian, they cried out to God. During that time, Gideon was threshing his wheat in the winepress so the Midianites wouldn't find his harvest and extract it from him. The Lord spoke to him, "The Lord is with you, O mighty man of valor" (Judges 6:12).

Gideon didn't think of himself as mighty. He was worried about his nation's problems. In verse 13, he asked the angel, "If the Lord is with us, why then has all this happened to us?" It is a common question asked by all humanity when problems arise. It can be a paralyzing place. Almost no one moves forward in life until they can quit obsessing about why the difficulty exists.

God didn't answer Gideon's question about why, but rather gave him an instruction for the future. Verse 14 says, "Go in this might of yours and save Israel from the hand of Midian; do not I send you?" God was working on Gideon's thinking, from being problem-oriented to becoming solution-minded.

Gideon answered with the excuse that his clan was the weakest in his tribe, and that he was the least in his father's house. Gideon was problem-minded and consumed with thinking of how weak his family was. When we read the rest of the story, we find that his mindset wasn't even correct, because his father had multiple bulls and at least 10 employees. There is no way that a family with over 10 employees is the weakest family around.

God kept helping Gideon's thinking, saying, "But I will be with you" (Judges 6:16).

Just like with Joshua, Gideon needed a mindset change. He had to believe God was with him, helping him accomplish what he'd been told to do. No one gets far in life or accomplishes much without having a positive way of thinking.

Some critics argue that we should not be so focused on success and accomplishments. They try to tell us we ought to be happy with where we are in life. Being content in life is important, but that does not mean we passively remain where we are. When Israel conquered enough land to live in peace and prosperity, Joshua asked them, "How long will you put off going in to take possession of the land, which the Lord, the God of your fathers, has given you?" (Joshua 18:3). Even though they were secure, they were still expected to advance further. In the New Testament, we are reminded, "But my righteous one shall live by faith, and if he shrinks back, my soul has no

SHRINKING, COASTING, OR NOT MOVING FORWARD IS *NEVER* ACCEPTABLE FOR GOD'S PEOPLE.

pleasure in him" (Heb. 10:38). Shrinking, coasting, or not moving forward is *never* acceptable for God's people. The Bible is full of examples of those who, "conquered kingdoms, enforced justice, obtained promises, stopped the mouths of lions, quenched the power of fire, escaped the edge of the sword, were made strong out of weakness" (Heb. 11:33–34) and so forth. And because of these examples, we are instructed to, "lay aside every weight, and sin . . . and run with endurance the race that is set before us" (Heb. 12:1).

A forward-looking, positive mindset is both biblical and critical to creating the future God wants for us. That's why God had to help Gideon change his way of thinking. Without it, Gideon wouldn't be able to do anything about the problems he and his nation were facing.

From a natural perspective, we see how thinking patterns influence people's lives and their future. Let me illustrate. There are millionaires who have downsized for a season in their life. When they move into a smaller house, they typically treat that house well, and often make continual small upgrades that leave the house in much better shape. In a couple of years, they can put that house on the market for top price and make a profit when it sells. People at the other end of the economic spectrum move into a larger home, and within a couple of years, they bring the quality of that home down to their level. The grass is allowed to have more weeds. Floors are treated roughly; walls and doors get damaged. They simply bring with them habits that rich people usually do not have, habits that devalue their home to their own personal level. Everyone influences most of their circumstances and brings them in line with the quality of their own thinking and habits.

If you surround yourself with people whose thinking processes you would like to imitate, you will begin to think the same way they do. Study closely how they think, their daily habits, how they respond to various situations in life, how they treat their homes, what their day looks like, how they bring up their kids, how they approach work, and so forth. If you will study and emulate their thought processes and habits, your future will mirror what their current life looks like.

Whatever your life looks like this year was created by your thought processes, habits, and actions in the last five years. If you don't make any changes in your thinking, your future will be the same as it is today. Sadly, most people live this way. They have a faint hope of something better, but they never change. If they never change how they think and act, their future won't change much. That is why most people live and die with a life that looks very much like their parents and the people they grew up around.

Sure, part of life is that events don't always go as planned. No one ever had a life where every little detail panned out exactly like they thought it would. Sometimes we find ourselves in situations that were beyond our own control. At other times we find ourselves in a mess we created by our own mistakes. But even in the hard seasons of life, our thought processes and attitudes can shorten or lengthen their duration. Even if things are taken from us, we still have the ability to control our thinking and attitude. In fact, our attitude is one of our freedoms that can never be taken away.

> EVEN IN THE HARD SEASONS OF LIFE, OUR THOUGHT PROCESSES AND ATTITUDES CAN SHORTEN OR LENGTHEN THEIR DURATION.

My grandparents experienced occupation by the Germans during World War II. One of my grandfathers was put to forced labor in Norway. Because of their stories, I always had a keen interest in the history of the war. One day, I visited one of the Nazi concentration camps and got a closer look at the atrocities which took place there. Throughout the tour, we learned of barbaric practices that took place at that site, and the utter shock of the cruelty exceeded what we had seen just a few minutes earlier. Towards the end, we finally stood inside one of the gas chambers where so many had been executed. The door shutting behind me is still one of those sobering experiences that no book, story, or movie can ever recreate. As I stood there as a visitor, the heart-wrenching cruelty and the brutality of evil became so much more real. It's hard to put into words the emotions I experienced. But amazingly, even with everything those prisoners endured, some survivors shared how they could still choose their attitude under the absolute worst of conditions and circumstances.

Viktor E. Frankl was one of those survivors and he wrote in his best-selling book, *Man's Search For Meaning*, "Everything can be taken from a man but one thing: the last of the human freedoms—to choose one's attitude in any given set of circumstances, to choose one's own way."

If he could choose his attitude while being degraded the way he was, what's stopping us from choosing a good attitude at any given moment? Let's choose to believe that God is a good God, that He wants us to have an abundant life, that He wants us to accomplish something, and that He is for us, with us, and in us. Never look at problems with despair, but with confidence. Think about solutions and believe you can make a better future for yourself and for those around you.

Remember, the psalmist said, ". . . on his law he meditates day and night . . . In all that he does, he prospers" (Ps. 1:2–3). The One who designed and created life knows what He is talking about. There truly is a way to prosper in everything.

Say What?

While thinking right is crucial, progress does not happen by just thinking. Sometimes positive-thinking motivational talks are just entertainment or edutainment. Fun sayings and motivational talk is fine, but at some point, the right thoughts need to be spoken.

Back in Joshua 1:8, we read, ". . . Keep this Book of the Law always on your lips . . ." Whatever someone thinks about becomes evident in what they say. A lover of football will inadvertently talk about football because they think about it regularly.

We need to think about Scripture so habitually that we inadvertently talk about the Word of God and biblical principles in our daily conversations. This goes beyond a list of verses taped to our bathroom mirror that we confess in the morning. It needs to become so much a part of us that it goes with us wherever we go.

EVEN THOUGH JOSHUA AND CALEB HAD WALKED TOGETHER WITH 10 DOUBTERS FOR 40 DAYS, THEY REFUSED TO BE INFLUENCED BY THEIR UNBELIEF.

When Joshua and Caleb came back with the other 10 spies from spying out the land in Numbers 13, the other spies talked about all the problems, how the cities were fortified, and the people in the land were very strong. They reached the conclusion that they could not take the land. But even though Joshua and Caleb had walked together with these 10 doubters for 40 days, they refused to be influenced by their unbelief. They reported to Moses, "Let us go up at once and occupy it, for we are well able to overcome it" (Num. 13:30). They must have spent so much time thinking about God's promise of taking the land, that even though people around them didn't believe and even though there really were giants in the land, they still spoke in accordance with God.

Later in life, long after Joshua and Caleb had entered the land, they reflected back on this time and Caleb told Joshua, "... when Moses the servant of the Lord sent me from Kadesh-barnea to spy out the land, and I brought him word again as it was in my heart" (Joshua 14:7).

So many people miss it by focusing on and speaking according to what they see in their circumstances or what their emotions are telling them in the moment. But those who meditate on the Word of God place it so deeply within their heart, they can speak from their hearts in times of adversity.

Many people, Christians included, just say whatever comes to their minds, whether it lines up with the Word of God or not. And then they wonder why their life is falling apart or their situation never improves. We can *never* forget that there is power in what we say! In the New Testament, James likened our tongues to a rudder on a large ship (James 3:4–5). Those massive ships in the ocean will go wherever the rudder directs them. In the same way, our lives will go according to what we speak with our tongues. I grew up around the ocean. I once had the opportunity to steer a larger ship. I noticed something very interesting.

When you turn the wheel of the ship, you won't notice any change of course for a while. The ship is so huge that it takes a while to turn, but it will if you keep the rudder steady at the new position. The same is true with changing how we talk. If we persist in speaking the right words, it surely will guide our future. We just have to make sure we don't fall back into old habits. The only way to keep that from happening is to keep on meditating on the Word of God and speaking it out.

Act

God's instructions to Joshua didn't end with meditating and speaking in line with God. In Joshua 1:8 He said, ". . . be careful to *do* according to all that is written in it. For then you will make your way prosperous, and then you will have good success."

Success comes from doing, and not just doing something, but doing the right thing.

In order for an airplane to take off, there are a lot of systems that need to be working properly. To name a few, the fuel and engine provide the necessary thrust. Radios provide necessary communication with airports on the ground and other aircraft in the sky to prevent collisions in heavily trafficked skies. There is also the navigational system that helps a pilot know where they are and map out the correct course for where they need to go.

In an aircraft, if the navigational system does not work well, you cannot compensate for it by installing a larger engine. If the engine is not getting enough fuel, having the latest navigational system will not compensate for a faulty engine.

Similarly, we have seen many that keep improving areas in their life where they are already strong. Most people I see fail to get ahead because they have problems in a particular area and don't do anything to fix it. There are lots of people who own a business and are great at selling their product, but have a problem with recruiting and managing employees. They can work on improving their sales skills further and that may help some, but it would be much more effective for them to fix their problem area and learn how to work together with employees. Similarly, there are companies that have phenomenal products and great teams of engineers, but really struggle with marketing and sales. Sometimes I have talked to the owners, and they can explain how they are pouring resources into developing enhancements to their products so that more customers will want what they offer. But if their marketing is poor, they would do better to overhaul their sales and marketing than to enhance an area where they are already successful.

That's why God told Joshua, ". . . be careful to do according to *all* that is written in it." The Bible has the answers to the issues of life. But too many only highlight the verses they like and keep reading those, while ignoring other instructions. No one can be an expert at everything. We all have areas where we are strong, but we need to be well rounded in a wide range of areas.

We see this from the Word as well. Samson was one of Israel's judges and he delivered the nation from the Philistines. He didn't have problems with physical strength or fighting off enemies, but he did have problems with women. Placing lust in good looks instead of being faithful to a wife with character and integrity became his downfall. Samson's life was cut short because there was a major area in his life where he refused to be a doer of what God told him to do.

> GOD PROMISED US SUCCESS FOR THIS SIMPLE REASON; HE GREATLY DESIRES US TO BE SUCCESSFUL.

In the New Testament, James wrote that we are to receive the word of God with humility and be careful not only to listen but also to do because, ". . . a doer who acts, he will be blessed in his doing" (James 1:25).

God promised us success for this simple reason; He greatly desires us to be successful. He instructed us to constantly *think* in line with His Word, to *say* what He said, and that we *do* everything He told us to do. All of our thinking, speaking, and doing will create our futures. But for those who think, speak, and act in line with God, the future will be one of success, harmony, peace, and satisfaction.

CHAPTER 4

Kick the Dependency Syndrome

In my travels around the world, I find people who wish they had more, who wish others would provide more for them, and wish life was easier than it is. Solomon described it:

> Proverbs 21:25–26
>
> 25 The desire of the sluggard kills him, for his hands refuse to labor.
>
> 26 All day long he craves and craves, but the righteous gives and does not hold back.

The poor will not work on producing anything of value, yet they keep on seeking and searching for money. They are looking for someone to provide for them without doing anything to earn the value they desire.

The dependency syndrome is when people look to others to be their source, avoiding personal responsibility by putting the responsibility for their life on other people. It has become a huge issue in many places around the world, particularly in poorer areas where well-meaning and good-hearted people have come to help the situation by providing for the needs of the poor.

I have plenty of experience seeing the extremes of poverty and the horrendous effect it has on people. I also have too much experience seeing how giving handouts to the poor only makes the problem worse. Kenyans are known for being very warm, welcoming, and hospitable. That has been my experience in traveling all over Kenya for the last 20 years. Even if they didn't have much, they would still honor their visitors and give them the best they had. But the sad part is whenever I travel to a part of Kenya where there have been lots of missionaries and many handouts given, the people are no longer looking to honor a guest. They have become more poor and are looking for the guests to give them another handout.

When I travel to some places where the international aid organizations have done lots of work, the dependency syndrome is at its worst. One time, we traveled into a remote town towards the South Sudan border with Kenya, an area where the United Nations has had a large operation for years in order to provide aid into South Sudan. At the time, we were training pastors with a mobile Bible school curriculum, and we would come into a town or village center, meet with all the pastors, and offer to provide training. We would pay all of our own bills as well as provide the instructors, books, and materials. The only two things we asked for was a small fee from each student so there would be some sort of commitment from them. If we didn't, we would have too many people come and go and it would be hard to bring them through a well laid out curriculum. Secondly, we asked the pastors to provide the venue for the training and suggested that they make one of their churches available so that no one had to incur further expenses.

This worked well everywhere we'd been, but in this area of foreign aid, the pastors came with a long list of complaints. For one, they were upset that we didn't provide a meal at our initial meeting. Giving them a traditional cup of tea wasn't enough. Secondly, they asked if we could provide a sitting allowance to come and listen when attending school. They were used to being paid an allowance for coming to attend the seminars that the foreign aid organizations were hosting. Third, if they were going to provide a venue, they would have to charge each student a fee for going to the latrine to relieve themselves. After all, they needed money to pay for someone to clean the latrine at the end of the day.

It's a sad story, but free handouts only create dependency and make poverty worse. It certainly is scriptural to help the poor, but we need to do it in a way that truly helps. Paul instructed Timothy to help those that were widows indeed and could not help themselves (see 1 Timothy 5).

I could share countless other stories like that, but what we need to learn is true success comes by thinking in line with God's Word in all areas of life. Dependency thinking is contrary to the Bible. Proverbs 12:11 tells us, "Whoever works his land will have plenty of bread, but he who follows worthless pursuits lacks sense."

All of us were born without anything, and we were utterly dependent. Growing up is all about learning to transition from being dependent to being independent, from being a consumer to a provider, and from being a taker to a giver. The truth is we all have something inside of us that would prefer to be dependent and have someone provide everything we need. Staying in a hammock by the beach with someone else to cook for us and provide coconuts all day, or spending lots of time on the golf course or with our favorite pastime can sound enticing to most everyone. But such desires are nothing but daydreams unless we learn to provide value to others. It is only when we provide value to society that society, in turn, is willing to reward us with leisure and comfort.

WE ALL FEEL THE DESIRE TO BE DEPENDENT ON OTHERS. THAT DESIRE ISN'T GOOD, AND IT'S NOT FROM GOD. KICK IT OUT!

This doesn't mean we shouldn't be willing to help others. The Bible tells us we should. But "others" should never be anyone's primary source. That's when the dependency syndrome takes over.

We all get tempted to want someone else to do the hard work for us. At times, we all feel the desire to be dependent on others. That desire isn't good, and it's not from God. Kick it out!

Don't Blame Externals

All of us grew up in an environment we did not choose. Some are born into unfortunate circumstances. Others are born with a silver spoon in their mouths, so to speak. Some parents can't afford to educate their children. Others have the means to send their kids to world-class institutions. Life does not seem to be fair. At the same time, if people are given the right knowledge, everyone has opportunities in life. Some might have to work harder, but the opportunities are there.

There have been many government and economic policies proposed to try to build some fairness into life. The debate between the political left and the political right still rages. Should we embrace socialism and ensure all people are on the same level? Or should we embrace individual freedom and make sure everyone has equal opportunities? Regardless of the philosophy, there is no country on earth where everything is fair. There are both rich and poor everywhere; there are both industrious and lazy people everywhere.

The one common factor is the tendency for everyone to point fingers. We point fingers at politicians who aren't doing enough. Some will blame their current situation on their upbringing, lack of education, insufficient parenting, and so on. It's very easy to place the responsibility for our current situation on other external factors that we don't have control over. The problem is, as long as we blame factors we can't control, we are doomed to remain in our current state. The good news is regardless of our current situation, we all have the opportunity to rise above where we are and live a better life.

Jim Stovall was diagnosed with macular degeneration at the age of 17, an eye disease that most often attacks the elderly. He considered dropping out of high school. Instead, he not only graduated from high school, but college as well. By the age of 29, he was totally blind. Many would have given up at this point and relied on others to help them get through life. But Jim Stovall never allowed his physical condition to hinder his mindset. Rather, he found a solution to one of the problems 13 million people like him had. Blind people were unable to watch TV, so he created television for the blind. That sounds like something impossible, and many laughed at his idea. But he worked hard, overcame many challenges, and today has built a television network for the blind, and is a multimillionaire. He has won numerous awards, including an Emmy, Humanitarian of the Year, and Entrepreneur of the Year.

Nick Vujicic is another example of one who is greatly disadvantaged. Born without any arms or legs, he couldn't run and play with other kids growing up. As a result, he struggled with depression and loneliness. Over time, his faith in God and a good group of people around him helped him change his thinking. As a result, Nick has become an author and a sought after motivational speaker and his hobbies include fishing, painting, and swimming

The principle we all need to learn is that poverty is not a lack of money. Poverty is a mental condition that results in the lack of money. No one can blame us for the situation we are born into. If you are born into poverty or a difficult family situation, it is not your fault. As a child, a person has limited control over these circumstances. As a person grows and develops, however, it is possible to get wisdom, grow in knowledge and understanding, and make something better out of their current situation. Not everyone has the same start in life, but everyone has a personal responsibility for what they do with their life.

THE PRINCIPLE WE ALL NEED TO LEARN IS THAT POVERTY IS NOT A LACK OF MONEY. POVERTY IS A MENTAL CONDITION THAT RESULTS IN THE LACK OF MONEY.

Where we are today in life is a result of the thought patterns, our words, and our actions in times past. As we discussed in a previous chapter, our tomorrow is created by the thought patterns, words, and actions we have today. For many, this is a heavy burden. We are responsible for our own lives, and no one owes us anything. We came into the world with nothing and should be thankful for everything we have. At the same time, this is also very liberating because it means I can get somewhere regardless of my current situation or external factors around me.

Having worked in Kenya for well over a decade, I can now take you to village after village where we have taught these principles and have seen people come out of poverty. Moving into success is doable even for those in the most dire situations.

Pastor Justus Kaloki in Vipingo, a remote village along Kenya's coast, is one of those examples. When he was going to our school, I found out he was working the night shift, coming to school during the day, preaching in his newly started church in the evening, and then going back to work. His willingness to add school to his already busy schedule made me want to see where he had started the church.

Vipingo was known as a poor area, and when I visited, I quickly saw why. No matter where I looked, I couldn't find any significant buildings or institutions, and the people I saw were poorly dressed, adults and kids alike. Pastor Kaloki started his church by renting half of a mud hut. It didn't look like much. At the service that evening, I think we had about 10 adults with several dozen kids, but I preached my heart out as if the crowd was large. Afterward, I encouraged the pastor the best I could, but drove away wondering how in the world he would survive as a pastor in that place.

A few years later, I heard that Pastor Kaloki was doing very well, that they had built a new church building, and the church members had donated a car to the pastor. I was surprised, because I knew that when I was there, the offering was $1 on Sunday, maybe $2 on a good Sunday. I needed to see this for myself. When I came, the congregation had grown, and I could tell by their demeanor and dress that there were people of means in the congregation.

I didn't recognize anyone, and asked the pastor, "Where are the people I preached to a few years ago?"

"They are still here," he said, "but they have changed so much, you can't recognize them."

Not only had the church grown in number, but the people had grown in means, and all the funds for both the building and the car—over $35,000—came from the members of the local congregation. I asked Pastor Kaloki, "How did this happen?" He looked at me and said, "We just implemented what you taught us, and started teaching the same to our congregation. The four most important areas were biblical economics, that is giving and receiving. Then, practical stewardship, how to budget and handle finances. Third, we taught on faith, how God would supply your needs and how to ask God for help. Lastly, we taught people work ethics." Then, he explained that the people who didn't have jobs started finding jobs. They did so well, that many got promotions. Those who didn't find jobs, started their own businesses and were doing very well. "When I started the church, people had no work and nothing to do. My problem now is that when I need volunteers for the church, everyone is already busy!"

These and other similar stories are what we hear from various parts of Kenya where we have taught what we are sharing with you in this book. When people are willing to learn and do something different with their lives, they will grow, and there will be no need for handout programs. Rather, Pastor Kaloki and his members have started many businesses that provide employment to the villagers, and they have also started a private Christian school in the community to give children a better opportunity than what the government can provide. Now, the parents in the church no longer think about orphanages or what program to send their kids to. They have the means to give them a good education. The best institutions in the village were started by the church, making the church a light and an example in the area.

Become a Resource

Most everyone walking the planet today wishes they had a higher income, more influence, or the ability to live a little more comfortably. This is true of the rich and poor alike. Those who believe the circumstances are the problem will often get involved in trying to change the externals. They may join political lobbies or unions to try to change laws or collectively try to negotiate a better salary from the employer. Working on changing the externals is usually a long road that results in changes that are too small. Unions typically negotiate small pay increases, but don't propel their members to new standards of living.

Here is a better principle that revolutionized my thinking. Whatever amount of money we earned last month is the exact amount our employer or customer was willing to pay for the product or service we offered. It is the very amount they perceived our product or service to be worth. We may not feel like the amount is fair. We may believe our service is worth more. But our feeling doesn't change the fact that our employer or customer paid the amount they thought our service or product was worth.

There is a sure and proven way to get a raise, whether we are employed or self employed. If we increase the value of what we provide, eventually we will be paid more. That is much more effective than engaging in political lobbying or union bargaining. If we put effort into increasing the value of our knowledge, skills, and efficiency (something we can all do), we will eventually be paid more. Personally, I would never want to work at a place that has a unionized workforce, because it means my pay is limited by the value of what my coworkers produce, and it removes my incentive for doing a better job.

In other words, looking for more money is the wrong way to go about things. No matter how much we wish, cry, or beg, it will not increase the value of what we are doing, nor will it help us add to society's total production value. But if we focus on becoming a better resource and a more valuable worker, then not only are we giving others a good reason to pay us more, but we also add to the value of society. Zig Ziglar summed it up perfectly when he said, "When you do more than you are paid to do, you will eventually be paid more for what you do."

Whether we are an employee or self employed, if we change our mindset, take the focus off the money, and seek to add value to the relationship, we will eventually find ourselves in a better position.

Start with doing all the basics well. Always show up a little early, dressed to impress, and with a great attitude. Then look to do your job excellently, better than an average worker would. Make sure you follow through on all the little promises you make. If you look to do a little more than everyone else, you do it with a smile, and continuously grow in knowledge in your field, you will be valuable to whoever is paying you.

The only way to make money is by adding value to somebody else. If you want to make *more* money, you must find a way to add *more* value to others.

Embrace Opportunity

One will not move forward by only looking at the past to determine who or what event caused us problems. Although we sometimes have to deal with trauma from the past in order to move forward, we cannot undo actions that were taken. History is what it is. At the same time, if we keep doing the same things we've always done, we can't expect our lives to change significantly. In order to move forward and improve our lives even more, we must look for opportunities to do something better than what we have been doing. Opportunities are found everywhere. All too often, though, they are disguised as hard work. Too many people are unwilling to change because it looks too hard, involves risk, or requires that we leave comfort for a little while. Most people never grow because they are looking for something easy to do.

OPPORTUNITIES ARE FOUND EVERYWHERE. ALL TOO OFTEN, THOUGH, THEY ARE DISGUISED AS HARD WORK.

Breaking out of the circle we are currently in is hardly ever easy, but it's necessary if we want to have better results.

I have seen lots of families with medium to low incomes struggle to make ends meet. Often, both mom and dad are working full days and have children to raise as well. It can be hectic and challenging to try to give the kids the best when finances are tight. There are not many, but I know a few families in this situation where either mom, dad, or sometimes both went back to school. They researched various careers, were honest with themselves about their abilities, explored schooling options, and checked the employment market to ensure there were good job opportunities available when their education was complete.

They found an opportunity and were determined to do the hard work. Going back to night school when you are already busy with a full-time job and a family is not easy. Most opportunities are difficult. It will require extra effort for a while before the benefits pay off. But I have watched several of these families, and noticed that they end up living better, more comfortable lives and are in a position to provide better opportunities for their children.

Another example is that of a traveling minister. Most would love to have more bookings in bigger churches. Larger churches usually have higher expectations from guest ministers. Yet, it is not uncommon for a minister to wish things were better without preparing *themselves* to be better. There are always opportunities to improve, but there are few who will put in the time or effort to make those improvements. Good pulpit communicators often spend a full workday or more per week in preparing their material. The average ones have the same opportunity, but usually aren't willing to make that kind of commitment.

In 2010 I was working two jobs, both as an IT director at Kenneth Hagin Ministries and as director of Bible colleges in Kenya. The job in Kenya didn't pay anything, and with a growing family, we were looking to supplement our income. We had been careful with spending money, and had a little equity in our home, but not much savings otherwise. Since we had built a good credit history with banks, we saw that it was possible to take out an equity loan on our home and use that cash as a down payment on another home. We bought a small 1,000 square foot (90 m²) home built in the 1950s. The bank had foreclosed on it and it wasn't liveable. I had maxed out what the bank would loan us, two kids to take care of, hardly any money or savings, two jobs, and I was under pressure to get this house remodeled so we could rent it out to tenants. It wasn't easy, but Tulsa had a decent rental market. I saw that this was an opportunity to make a little rental income and to build some extra equity over time. One day as my wife and I were working on remodeling, I was crawling under the home to do some work in the crawl space. As I was laying there on the ground and staring up at the floor to this old house thinking *What kind of crazy project have I gotten myself into?* I was exhausted, dirty, hadn't seen my kids much that weekend, and felt like quitting. That old, little home became the beginning of us taking opportunities to grow and stretch financially. We ended up selling this house several years later, and it enabled us to move into bigger financial opportunities. It was scary to undertake the project when we started, and we spent many hours being frustrated over the remodeling process or by the tenants we had, but if we hadn't taken the opportunity, we would not have been able to move ahead financially.

> IF YOU WANT TO GROW AND DO WELL IN LIFE, YOU HAVE TO LEARN TO EMBRACE OPPORTUNITY.

If you want to grow and do well in life, you have to learn to embrace opportunity. Remember, an opportunity to make money is also an opportunity to add value to someone else's life. When you add value to someone else, you improve society. In order to improve society, it requires that we as individuals take the opportunities available and work to make others' lives better. In business, a good deal is always a win for everyone involved. Learn to create wins for others in society, be a giver, and you will be rewarded yourself.

Solomon's words from Proverbs 12:11 bear repeating here, "Whoever works his land will have plenty of bread, but he who follows worthless pursuits lacks sense." In other words, if you embrace the available opportunities, your provision will not be a problem. Don't look for fairytale opportunities that are easy, have high return, but never show up.

Solomon actually went even further when he said, "The people curse him who holds back grain, but a blessing is on the head of him who sells it" (Prov. 11:26).

I have seen many who will only grow to the place where they can live comfortably themselves. When they reach that place, they stay there instead of growing further so that they can be a blessing to other people.

In my travels in East Africa, I have seen many landowners and farmers who own larger tracts of land, but will only grow crops on a small portion that yields a harvest which enables them to live comfortably. There isn't much left over to sell or to help neighbors. Solomon, in his wisdom, wrote that it is a curse to hold back grain in this way, but there is a blessing for those who produce enough to sell to others. Someone who owns 10 acres of land should not produce only one or two acres. They should take the opportunity to produce the other eight or nine acres as well so they can bless others.

This same mentality is all over the Western world too. Once we have a job that is good enough to live a comfortable life, our goals and dreams are about vacation. I have heard many conversations from people returning to work the first day after a vacation, and their talk is about where they plan on going for their next vacation.

It simply isn't right to sit and watch opportunities pass us by. When we are passive, we actually rob our neighbors and refuse to produce something of value that we should be adding to their lives. We need to shake off laziness and stop only thinking about ourselves. Instead, we need to keep growing and producing even after we have reached a place of being comfortable.

When Caleb was 85 years old, Israel had crossed the Jordan about five years earlier and settled in the new promised land. Yet, instead of getting comfortable, Caleb wanted to acquire Hebron, so he went to Joshua and said, "I am still as strong today as I was in the day that Moses sent me; my strength now is as my strength was then, for war and for going and coming. So now give me this hill country of which the Lord spoke . . . the Lord will be with me, and I shall drive them out just as the Lord said" (Joshua 14:11–12).

Joshua warned the people of Israel about passivity and not wanting to take on new opportunities once they had gotten comfortable. When you have been through slavery in Egypt, seen the hand of God deliver through the Red Sea, seen the daily manna and how God provided in the midst of a desert of impossibilities, when you have faced the impossible city of Jericho and yet God delivered—when you have been through all that and finally are at the point where you have your own land, your own fields, and have the ability to live in peace and comfort, it becomes easy to want to settle down for a while. Yet, at this point Joshua tells them, "How long will you put off going in to take possession of the land, which the Lord, the God of your fathers, has given you?" (Joshua 18:3).

Thankfully, the nation of Israel listened to Joshua and they didn't settle for what they had but continued taking more of the land God had promised them. The Bible then says that everything the Lord promised them had come to pass (Joshua 21:45). God is good, and His promises *do* come to pass, but those who are busy doing what He told them to do end up experiencing God at work in their lives, even seeing Him intervene in the course of life and nature.

At Joshua's farewell speech, when "the Lord had given rest to Israel from all their surrounding enemies," he once again reminded the people that they needed to remember what God told them in the beginning, to "be very strong to keep and to do all that is written in the Book of the Law of Moses, turning aside from it neither to the right hand nor to the left" (Joshua 23:1, 6). In the following verses, he also reminded them that there was more land to inherit, that they should not mix with the surrounding nations, but take the opportunity and conquer them. Being comfortable is no excuse for not taking further opportunities and advancing in life.

As a young boy growing up in Norway, I was accustomed to every single yard being filled with fruit trees, berries, and potatoes. You could be sure that every fall, all the kids in the street would go and hunt for the best apples or plums from a neighbor's yard on their walk to and from school. I remember my grandmother carefully picking the fruit and berries and making them into delicious fruit drinks or yummy fruit spread. There was not a single yard without at least one apple tree. To me, that was just what I was used to growing up and I just saw that as normal. In reality, this all stemmed from the hardships during World War II. Norway was occupied by the Germans, and food was rationed and scarce. From that, my grandparent's generation would farm the yard around their houses. Any patch found was used to plant potatoes, berries, apples, plums and so forth. I have noticed that almost everyone in my grandparents generation was more than willing to take every small opportunity they could find. Virtually everyone in that generation was more than able to take care of themselves and their families. That is how it is in life. When we embrace opportunity, we will be a blessing to others and we will be blessed ourselves.

CHAPTER 5

Becoming Gold

Within every one of us, there is a gold waiting to be mined. Years ago, I visited a gold mine in Colorado. Deep below the surface, amongst rock, dust, and darkness, we found gold in its original, raw form. It looked so different from the gold you see in finished jewelry that a professional miner had to point it out to us and explain what to look for to find it. Much of the gold was still left in that old mine, but some had been mined out and gone through a lengthy process and eventually found its way into fine Swiss Rolex watches. Refining gold is a tough process that requires a lot of heat and energy. The rock containing the gold gets crushed, and the low value stuff gets removed, before the high content rock goes into a furnace under extreme temperatures. There, the gold will melt and is further separated from other minerals and chaff. The material that makes it out of the furnace becomes very high in value and can be sold at great prices, but the process to become a part used in a Rolex is far from finished yet. At the Rolex factory in Switzerland, the raw material will still spend another year going through many difficult and high precision processes before they are turned into beautiful and highly durable watches that will be passed on from generation to generation.

"MORE GOLD HAS BEEN MINED FROM THE THOUGHTS OF MEN THAN HAS BEEN TAKEN FROM THE EARTH." -NAPOLEON HILL

The vast majority of the material from the original gold mine in Colorado will exit the process along the way and never reach the full value of its potential. But for each phase that the gold successfully goes through, its value will increase. Such is the gold that is found within each and every one of us.

Society is filled with average people. The average person surrounds themselves with average people. Yet, the average person has a desire to see their lives come to an above-average level. A leader will always do things differently. A leader does not follow the masses of society. In order for others to want to follow, the leader must inherently have qualities that others want to follow. There must be thinking processes, habits, and behavioral patterns the average person considers worth following. When you are full of great thinking, great habits, and great action, the average person will look at you like a gold nugget buried in the midst of an average society. You must be willing to, over a period of time, undergo some heat, pressure, and energy refining yourself.

It is human nature to always look for the easiest way. At a place of employment, most workers do roughly what is expected, not much less and not much more. When work is finished, most look to indulge in what they enjoy doing. They provide just enough value to society while they work to keep their job and put food on their table, yet are looking to maximize their personal pleasure when they clock out for the day. Such thinking must be kicked to the curb if you want to be a gold nugget. But if a person has lived like that for years, or maybe grew up in a household where that was the way of thinking, it will take time to replace those thinking patterns and habits. Gold doesn't shine for only eight hours a day. Gold remains the same 24 hours. Those that lead do not spend every evening being entertained. They either keep working or they spend time, money, and energy learning to be better.

There are those who don't even have average habits. People with a poverty mindset will blame others for their problems, complain about their situation in life, and often feel sorry for themselves. It is absolutely true that life isn't fair, society is full of problems, and many are in situations they didn't cause. But a poverty mentality causes passivity and makes the problem even worse for the poor person. So, whether you look in a slum in Nairobi, a poor neighborhood in Mississippi, or a welfare recipient in Europe, the thinking is typically the same. You usually find all kinds of clutter in their homes, including collections of all sorts of junk that they don't use and nobody wants to use. And the simplest of maintenance issues are never taken care of. But they all have a television and a phone with a Facebook account. They spend time and money on cheap entertainment, but won't fix things that are out of order.

"SUCCESS COMES TO THOSE WHO HAVE AN ENTIRE MOUNTAIN OF GOLD THAT THEY CONTINUALLY MINE, NOT THOSE WHO FIND ONE NUGGET AND TRY TO LIVE ON IT FOR FIFTY YEARS." -JOHN C. MAXWELL

Employers don't want to hire them, because they have thinking patterns that do not add to the value of a company. These people have to learn to build a habit to consistently get up on time, show up on time, look presentable when they arrive, and show up with a good attitude. Not only that, but they need to be ready to serve someone for eight hours and have a good attitude their entire shift. But again, it will take time for them to replace their old thinking patterns and habits. But going from poverty to average is available for anyone who is willing enough to change. The desire has to be big enough that they will actually make the necessary adjustments.

As I am writing this, I am sitting in a hotel in Lagos, Nigeria. A sharp looking flight crew from Qatar Airways just arrived, all looking very professional. In a few minute's time, they have gone to their rooms and changed into casual clothes and are enjoying themselves in the restaurant after a long flight. If I hadn't watched them come into the hotel in uniform, I would never have guessed they were professionals. They are now acting like ordinary people in casual middle-class clothes. Some are wearing shorts with t-shirts that do not match and sandals. There's nothing wrong with that, but they are not presenting themselves in a way where a business person would strike up a conversation. They are off duty and focused on entertaining themselves. I am in the same restaurant on an off day and have the same opportunity to relax and enjoy myself. Instead, I am busy writing this book. My clothes are comfortable but not too casual. I have on comfortable business slacks and a nicer short-sleeved shirt. For one, I never know who might show up in the same restaurant, or there might be some other business people around I strike a conversation with. Besides, hotel staff tend to give better service to those who present themselves better. I would have preferred to wear my shorts and t-shirt, but I left them in the room. I am sacrificing a little bit of comfort in order to make sure I can take advantage of an opportunity, should it arise. This may sound like a small, simple example, but when you refine gold, you have to look for the small imperfections and work on getting them out. There is a price to pay to go higher in life.

Each and every day, we make hundreds, if not thousands of small decisions. How do you hold your knife and fork? How do you treat the napkin on your table? How do you treat a total stranger walking by? Then there are larger decisions. How do you plan your day? How do you prioritize the tasks of your day and make sure the most important things get done? Around the family dinner table, do you purposefully guide productive conversations? Do you make sure everyone is doing well, help resolve any challenges people had that day, and then continue the conversation about visions, dreams, or maybe a life lesson everyone can learn from? Or do you just talk about news, the latest fad, or gossip about other people like most average people do? These are all habits, and you will need to go through your everyday life, analyze your thought processes and habits, and, one by one, go through them and upgrade them if you want to go from average to gold. The day you stop the journey of making constant improvements, that will be the day you set the level you will live on for the rest of your life. There is no glass ceiling or cap to how far you can go. You only set that cap the day you think *I am not willing to grow further, because I would rather have my current comfort level than to go through the pain of improving more habits and growing further.*

We all have the potential to be gold, but there is a price to pay.

Continuous Learning

Without counsel, plans go awry, but in the multitude of counselors they are established.

-Proverbs 15:22 (NKJV)

One of the great hallmarks of successful people is they are continuous learners. They don't stop learning when education ends. They are not afraid of getting help, but have lifelong habits of wanting to grow, and actively seek out advice, mentors, and books in areas they want to improve.

In business school at Oral Roberts University, we had some phenomenal professors. Dr. Eugene Swearingen had a long resume from a successful career before he retired and served on the faculty at the university for free. Every weekday, he would read a new book. He had developed a habit of speedreading and would spend an hour or two going through a new book every weeknight. He read 250 books a year. He then told his students about the best books available on the subjects of management, leadership, and entrepreneurship.

When I graduated with a master's degree in business administration, I had a pretty good overview of the field of management and leadership, but wanted to continue to learn. It was frustrating because I had a hard time finding any books with information I hadn't already learned. So I quit reading. I felt like I was already at the cutting edge of new information. After about 10 years, I started looking at various articles and found terminology and concepts I did not know about. So I started checking up on the fields of management and leadership. I quickly realized that everything I knew was outdated by about 10 years. So I started reading again.

I know all too many people who studied business, but their knowledge level ended when their studies did, and the world has long ago passed them. These people never become leaders. They settle at a level where they have become comfortable.

Pioneers, Settlers, and Museum Keepers

There are three kinds of people in the world; pioneers, settlers, and museum keepers. The pioneers are the ones who go ahead of others, try new things, take risks, and continue learning. The settlers are the ones who watch the pioneers and copy the best ideas from them. They do make progress, but they don't take much risk, and they always wait until something new becomes mainstream before they embrace it. Museum keepers are those who never want to change. They like the status quo and would rather dwell on memories of the past than to think of new ideas. They are hard to help, unless the pain of staying behind gets so bad they reluctantly make some changes.

But the interesting thing is that every one of the pioneers automatically becomes settlers and museum keepers if they stop growing and learning. That's why every leader is always a reader or a learner. If they don't read and learn, others will soon pass them by and they will cease to be a leader. As a leader, unless you keep learning and growing, it won't be long before your best followers outgrow you and then begin following more advanced leaders or they will branch out on their own.

There are many ways to learn and grow. It's been said that "Readers are leaders," but that's not always the case. If you are reading purely for pleasure, you aren't really growing. Unless we are reading for growth and action, our reading is simply entertainment. Real leaders always look at the areas where they need to improve, and then purposefully find resources to help them in that area. Leaders make growth a habit, and the information they learn, they put into practice. Knowledge not acted upon merely becomes useless information. News, stories, and actually lots of business books fall in this category. So much of what is written today is written to sell and entertain, so that it's hard to find books that are actually beneficial. Find those who are really good at the field you want to learn in, then ask them what resources they would recommend. Usually, they will be happy to point you in the right direction.

You have to implement what you read, instead of just reading for pleasure. Some business books are written for pleasure, because pleasure is often easier to sell than a book full of practical instructions. This is why so many business books are more motivational entertainment than they are educational growth material. It takes energy to read a quality book in an area where you want to grow. As you read, you will need to stop and absorb the content, look at how you can better your life, and implement the ideas you are reading about.

Personally, I don't have a natural inclination to enjoy reading. I ought to read 50 books per year, but I only read between 15 to 20. So it becomes more important that I read the *right* books, books that will help me grow. Here is how I select books to read. First, I select the areas where I need to grow. Second, I start looking for the best books available on those subjects. I don't have time to read mediocre books. Those who feed on mediocre books will end up with mediocre results. So I check reviews and also ask those who are ahead of me in the area I need to grow and inquire about the best books.

Becoming gold takes time—it is a continual process of refining and improving, of learning, and of growing. But if you will remain persistent in always making small improvements, others will eventually look at you as a gold mine.

CHAPTER 6

What About the Money?

The Balance

Money Isn't Everything

"Money isn't everything, but everything else can be bought with money."

This anonymous, yet funny quote is more true than many want to admit. Life is about so much more than money, but because this world's system operates on money, a healthy perspective on finances is required for our success and well being.

Certainly, everything cannot be bought with money. Good relationships are worth much more than what money can buy. No amount of money can compare to having peace and harmony in the family. Yet, in almost all areas of life, the right use of money can help. Good stewardship of finances can help build good relationships, and it can also help with peace and harmony in the family. Money isn't everything, but it can help with almost everything.

All throughout Africa, I have seen countless children who don't own much, but their lives are full of play and laughter. In remote areas, where there wouldn't be much to buy if you had money, I have seen adults contently talking about life in the cool of the day. Money certainly isn't everything and having much of it certainly does not guarantee happiness.

Money Is a Tool That Amplifies Your Character

Money is a tool to get something accomplished. Money on its own does not solve problems, but it can be part of the solution to most. Proper use of money can help mend relationships, it can help provide health for those who are sick, and it can purchase knowledge and education for those who need wisdom.

Money in itself is neither good nor evil. It is a tool that can be used for good or evil purposes. Money is a good amplifier of character. Find someone who doesn't have too much and give them a million dollars and watch what they do with it. You will very quickly find out if they are selfish or good stewards, whether they use money for good or for evil. Their character was there the whole time, but with money, it will be amplified for everyone to see so much easier. Make sure your character is right, that you want to be a steward of finances for the right reasons, and then view money as a tool to accomplish God's purpose in your life.

A Scriptural Balance

Throughout Scripture, we find instructions about money. When we look at these verses in their entirety, roughly half discuss how to be blessed and to increase, and the other half warn about being money-minded and remind us of things more important than money. The whole counsel of Scripture on finances clearly illustrate the need for balance about money.

We find this balance in the Old Testament. Solomon wrote, "A slack hand causes poverty, but the hand of the diligent makes rich" (Prov.10:4) and, "Do not toil to acquire wealth; be discerning enough to desist" (Prov. 23:4).

We do need to work in order to have money. There are those who are too lazy to ever make it very far in life. Then there are those who are obsessed with making money, their life centers around their work, career, or business, and they miss out on the things that really matter. But we are not to fret, worry, or work overly hard to chase money. Money is important, but it needs to have the right place. It should be our servant, not our master.

DON'T CHASE MONEY, BUT DO MANAGE MONEY. The New Testament teaches the same balance. Paul wrote to Timothy, "Those who desire to be rich fall into temptation, into a snare, into many senseless and harmful desires that plunge people into ruin and destruction. For the love of money is a root of all kinds of evils" (1 Tim. 6:9–10).

Money isn't everything. And those who love money for the sake of having more will be full of greed and never find contentment. Yet, there isn't anything wrong with having much money. If having a lot of money is wrong, the Bible wouldn't be full of instructions on how to be blessed and prosperous. Even the garden of Eden was supplied with gold, and the gold of that land was good (Gen. 2:10–14). But with money, lots of opportunities will arise, and so the Bible is full of warnings to those who have much money. One example is 1 Timothy 6:17 where Paul wrote, "As for the rich in this present age, charge them not to be haughty, nor to set their hopes on the uncertainty of riches, but on God, who richly provides us with everything to enjoy."

Spiritual Stewardship

In the area of finances, we see two areas that need to be balanced. There is a real spiritual side to God blessing us financially. And there are also some natural stewardship principles that are necessary. Personally,

I see lots of people who may be doing good in one of these areas, but could really use some help in the other.

Stewardship

When God created us, He created us to subdue the earth and rule over everything in it (Gen. 1:28). Adam and Eve were to work and till the garden. They were to be good stewards of what God created. Later in the Old Testament, the Lord says, "For every beast of the forest is mine, the cattle on a thousand hills" (Ps. 50:10).

Ultimately, all of creation owes everything to God. We need to live life with the mindset that we are stewards of what God has entrusted to us. With this mentality, it becomes easier to be thankful for what we have, and helps us deal with greed and entitlement that so easily creep into our thinking.

In Matthew 25, Jesus likens this world and the kingdom of God to a man going on a journey and entrusting everything—all his property and the management of it—to his servants. Those who managed well what they had been entrusted with would receive promotions when he came back.

We all are under the lordship of God. The only true way to live a successful, deeply meaningful life is by being obedient to what He has told us to do and managing what He has entrusted us with.

Supernatural Blessings

In following the Lord's instructions, there are supernatural blessings that come our way; blessings that are beyond what is naturally possible.

Proverbs 10:22

"The blessing of the Lord makes rich, and he adds no sorrow with it."

Proverbs 3:9–10

"Honor the Lord with your wealth and with the firstfruits of all your produce; then your barns will be filled with plenty, and your vats will be bursting with wine."

In the old Mosaic covenant, the Lord promised to bless His people. His hand would be upon them to the point that they were to lead all the nations around them.

Deuteronomy 28:11–12

"And the Lord will make you abound in prosperity, in the fruit of your womb and in the fruit of your livestock and in the fruit of your ground, within the land that the Lord swore to your fathers to give you. The Lord will open to you his good treasury, the heavens, to give the rain to your land in its season and to bless all the work of your hands. And you shall lend to many nations, but you shall not borrow."

Some will argue that this blessing is only in the Old Covenant. But long before the Mosaic covenant, God gave this promise to Abraham, when he said:

Genesis 12:2–3

"And I will make of you a great nation, and I will bless you and make your name great, so that you will be a blessing. I will bless those who bless you, and him who dishonors you I will curse, and in you all the families of the earth shall be blessed."

Whether we look at Abraham or the nation of Israel, God's will was always that His blessing would be upon His people. The blessing of Abraham came to pass, "Now Abram was very rich in livestock, in silver, and in gold" (Gen. 13:2). The blessing of Abraham is much more than just personal wealth for himself. He was known as a friend of God (2 Chr. 20:7; James 2:23). Both he and Sarah were healed and Isaac was born, and he became a great blessing to a great number of people. In him, all the nations of the earth have been blessed. The blessing of God upon Abraham touched all areas of his life, and it caused Abraham to be an example and a positive influence to lots of people around him.

Again, this blessing of the Lord isn't just an Old Testament reality. Paul writes to the Galatian church that this blessing of Abraham is for all believers, for "in Christ Jesus the blessing of Abraham might come to the Gentiles" (Gal. 3:14). In other words, when Christ came, He took all of the blessings that were to be upon Abraham and He made them available to anyone who would believe in Him. Not only did Christ save mankind and give us a way to heaven, but He provided a real blessing that touches all areas of our lives and enables us to be a positive influence to everyone around us.

Romans 8:32

He who did not spare his own Son but gave him up for us all, how will he not also with him graciously give us all things?

Around AD 56, Paul was collecting an offering from the churches in Greece to help with the famine situation in Jerusalem. He wrote plainly to the Corinthians, "For you know the grace of our Lord Jesus Christ, that though he was rich, yet for your sake he became poor, so that you by his poverty might become rich" (2 Cor. 8:9). That is not referencing some intangible spiritual blessing. The entire context of 2 Corinthians 8 and 9 is about finances, and Scripture plainly teaches that Christ's sacrifice includes the payment for our prosperity.

There indeed are supernatural blessings that God wants to bestow on His people, both under the Old Covenant and under the New Covenant. There is a real genuine blessing of the Lord, and this blessing comes from honoring God and placing Him first.

Generosity

During high school, I became aware that God wanted me to attend Bible college, and at some point, enter ministry. I also knew I was to get a professional degree from Oral Roberts University, but I should go to Bible college first. That meant I would come to ORU as a non-traditional student, and there would be fewer opportunities for scholarships.

I had no promises from my parents that they would pay, and I wondered greatly how college would be paid for, but I obeyed God and went to Rhema Bible Training College in Broken Arrow, Oklahoma, first. While at Rhema, I got my first job working an entry-level position in one of the fast food chains. In Bible college, after studying God's promises of provision, I told God, "At the end of this school year, I will take everything I have been able to save up, completely empty my bank account, and give it all to you." Throughout that year, at times it was tempting to not work as hard. After all, I was going to give away all my money anyway. Towards the end of that year, I battled with my mind, because I really needed much more than what I had in order to attend ORU. If I would just keep what I had and work some insane hours through the entire summer break, I would almost have enough to pay for the fall semester. But instead of giving in to natural reason, I kept my promise and gave away everything I had. It was about $1,700. That summer I did work, but there was no way I would make enough money to pay for school. But I kept believing in the blessing of God. To make a long story short, by the end of the year, I received grants and scholarships that paid for absolutely all of my entire bachelor degree. I didn't have to pay one penny!

There are real, supernatural blessings in following God, obeying Him, and being extravagantly generous. God's blessing is a spiritual reality, and it doesn't work like natural-minded people think it should. There is a true blessing in being a giver. Had I not followed through on my promise to give everything I had to God, I know I wouldn't have received those grants and scholarships.

Being generous is about so much more than giving money to the church. Truly content people are givers at heart. They don't just give money, but are generous with forgiveness and offering help of various kinds.

In terms of giving, we often hear Luke 6:38 quoted, "Give and it will be given to you. Good measure, pressed down, shaken together, running over, will be put into your lap. For with the measure you use it will be measured back to you." These promises are absolutely true, but the context here is not about giving in a church offering. The context is to not judge, to not condemn, to forgive, and also to give. Generosity is so much more than money, and the giving of finances is so much more than just putting money in the church offering.

Attitude Adjustments in Giving

I have been a giver all my life and had faithfully given tithes and offerings. But even though I was a giver, I still loved receiving more than giving. And there were many times I wondered why I wasn't receiving like the Bible promised. Thankfully, I had enough sense to know that God didn't lie. I knew His Word was, is, and always will be true, so the problem could not be with Him or His promises. That only left one option—me. The trouble with all too many Christians is they only believe parts of the Bible. Then, when certain things don't seem to work for them, they decide to follow the world's wisdom instead of pressing in to better understand what God really said.

So, instead of relying on what other people said about biblical giving and receiving, I dug deeper and studied more of the scriptures on finances, giving, and receiving. In studying Paul's planned collection in Greece for the poor in Jerusalem in 2 Corinthians 8 and 9, I discovered a few nuggets that really helped me.

Paul wrote in 2 Corinthians 9:6, "The point is this: whoever sows sparingly will also reap sparingly, and whoever sows bountifully will also reap bountifully." What we receive has more to do with how we sow than how we harvest. For a farmer, the process of sowing requires more thought and careful work than the act of harvesting. Whenever a harvest goes wrong, a farmer will go back to the time of sowing and analyze what happened to the seed up to the time of the harvest. Very often, if a farmer is having too small of a harvest, he will need to increase his sowing efforts in order to produce a better harvest.

WHAT WE RECEIVE HAS MORE TO DO WITH HOW WE SOW THAN HOW WE HARVEST.

Paul continued in verse 7, "Each one must give as he has decided in his heart, not reluctantly or under compulsion, for God loves a cheerful giver."

Let's look at this verse from a few translations to paint a better picture of what Paul was saying.

"You should each give, then, as you have decided, not with regret or out of a sense of duty . . ." (GNB).

"Let everyone give as his heart tells him . . ." (Phillips).

"Each man should give as he has decided in his heart. He should not give, wishing he could keep it. Or he should not give if he feels he has to give. God loves a man who gives because he wants to give" (NLV).

It was clear to me what the problem was. I had been giving willingly for years, but most often it was with a sense of duty, not because I necessarily wanted to give.

Once I noticed my error, I made some adjustments. I started enjoying the very act of giving. It was no longer a duty. I started rejoicing in being able to help others and seeing them blessed. When our true desire is to see others blessed, there is a real joy in giving. I would continually seek opportunities to sow and regularly ask the Lord where to give and how much. Instead of regretting what I had given, I started rejoicing because I was obedient.

Because of this small adjustment in attitude, I started seeing a big difference in what was coming in. Adjusting my sowing greatly affected my receiving.

Jesus said, "It is more blessed to give than to receive" (Acts 20:35).

Much, much more could be written about generosity and giving. An exhaustive study of this is beyond the scope of this book, so you may want to take a look at the recommended resources at the end of this book if you'd like to study this further.

Natural Stewardship

There Is More to Money Than Just Giving

There is a real spiritual blessing on giving. But while the blessing of God is real, there are also natural stewardship principles regarding finances that cannot be ignored.

I have seen many Christians who give, but seem to remain poor. Often, the problem is with how they give. They do it so reluctantly that there is no blessing in it. But I have seen some who are good givers, God blesses them, but they have such poor budgeting, spending, and saving habits that their higher income still doesn't produce too much for them.

I remember one pastor sharing how he had asked God for an additional amount of money for something he wanted to buy. He prayed and believed, but time went and his prayer seemed unanswered. So he went back and asked God about it. God told him to add up all the small extra amounts people had given to him over the past year. To his surprise, those small amounts added up to the larger amount he had asked for. But each time he received a smaller amount, he spent it on something small. God had answered his prayer, but his lack of self discipline in the area of budgeting, spending, and saving had kept him from enjoying God's answer to him.

There are others I know personally who have relatively high incomes. Yet, they are also high spenders and do not save much. Because they don't save, they are unable to take advantage of investment and other financial opportunities.

The Blessing of Opportunity

The primary way that the Lord blesses us is by making opportunities available and blessing the work of our hands.

Many quote Malachi 3:10–11, which says, "'Bring the whole tithe into the storehouse, that there may be food in my house. Test me in this,' says the Lord Almighty, 'and see if I will not throw open the floodgates of heaven and pour out so much blessing that there will not be room enough to store it. I will prevent pests from devouring your crops, and the vines in your fields will not drop their fruit before it is ripe,' says the Lord Almighty" (NIV).

So often, we hear emphasis put on the giving part of these verses. And it seems that so many have the mentality that if we will just give, God will bless, and then our bank accounts will magically be filled. But these verses were written to a predominantly agricultural society. When it talks of the windows of heaven opening, God did not mean that the grain would pour out of the sky into their barns. No, no, no! They were to give to God's house, yes. But the people still had to sow the seed into their farms. They still had to till the ground. And when there was harvest time, they still had to work to collect all the produce into their barns. They still had to do all of that natural work. God never intended sowing and reaping to be some sort of magical lottery where we no longer have responsibilities or need to do any work.

But giving to God and putting Him first will open spiritual blessings. God will bless the work of our hands and see to it that our crops are bountiful.

Opportunity and Preparedness

Prosperity happens when opportunity and preparedness meet. Some people have to pass up marvelous real estate deals because they never saved enough for a good down payment at the closing table. Often, your sowing opens up opportunities for you, but you have to use some natural saving principles if you are going to be prepared for the opportunities. Likewise, you never will be able to harvest 100 acres of wheat if you never had the seed to sow into the field to begin with.

PROSPERITY HAPPENS WHEN OPPORTUNITY AND PREPAREDNESS MEET.

Solomon said a few things about this side of finances. In Proverbs 13:11, he wrote, "Wealth gained hastily will dwindle, but whoever gathers little by little will increase it."

This means you must have a saving habit built into your financial life. Too many people want to put off saving until they have a higher income. But if you put an axe to your spending, live on a lower level for a while, and save your money, you can eventually invest it to produce more income. Keep doing this over a period of time, and you will enjoy financial freedom.

Solomon later wrote, "Whoever loves pleasure will be a poor man; he who loves wine and oil will not be rich" (Prov. 21:17).

Lovers of pleasure are spenders. They want the benefit now. You won't ever reach maturity if you won't learn to put off gratification and do the hard work now of saving and investing.

If we don't learn to save, we won't be prepared when opportunities come. To really be prepared, we have to save, and we have to acquire the knowledge to take advantage of the opportunity. Saving and learning are powerful tools to make progress in life.

Budgeting, Spending, Saving, and Investing

There are four basic things to do with money. You can spend it, give it, save it, and invest it. All four need to be understood and balanced. To go far, you have to minimize spending and focus on giving, saving, and investing.

Budgeting is an important aspect as well. I can't stress enough the importance of creating a budget and sticking to it.. There are many resources available on how to budget personal finances. I have included a few of them at the end of this book.

Here are just a few tips:

1) Most resources available on natural stewardship and budgeting do not understand the spiritual principles and the power of giving and receiving. Most resources that are great on the spiritual side

of giving and receiving say very little about natural stewardship. Study both sides, take the best of each, and you will be far ahead of most people.

2) If you don't have a budget, a good way to start is by taking one month and writing down everything you spend money on and organize it into categories. Some categories you can use are Giving, Savings, Education and Self Improvement, Housing Payment (mortgage or rent), Utilities, Food and Household, Car and Transportation, Children (Daycare, Education, Activities, etc.), Entertainment and Eating Out, and Clothing. Once you know where your money is going, you can make adjustments and put together a budget. The categories are roughly in order of importance. You generally want to increase your areas of giving, savings, and education/self improvement. Those areas will help you invest and create a larger cash flow over time. You do this by reducing what you spend on areas that do not help you produce income.

3) In terms of savings, know that the rich tend to decide what they want to save first, and then figure out how to live on the rest. The poor tend to spend first, then try to figure out how to save some from what is left over. In other words, savings will never happen unless it is made a priority.

4) Your financial situation can be improved by being more frugal in your spending or by increasing the flow of cash coming in. I know people who are very frugal and good with managing their money, but they don't know how to increase cash flow. Then there are those who know how to make money, but don't control their spending very well. The rich generally are very good at controlling spending, but they understand that you need to spend more time and energy on activities that increase cash flow.

5) It takes money to learn and grow. You need finances set aside for this. Books, classes, financial advisers, coaches, and the like do not come free. Yet, no one grows completely on their own without investing both time and money into these areas.

6) Buy value. In almost everything you buy, the cheapest items are so poorly made that they soon break and are more expensive in the long run because you have to purchase replacements. The most expensive items aren't necessarily made better. You are usually paying dearly for the latest fad or the name on the product. Both of these are true whether you are shopping for shoes or cars. Cheap shoes and cars are really expensive because the shoes fall apart soon and the car will have lots of expensive repairs. The most expensive shoes and cars look really nice, but won't really outlast shoes and cars that are good quality and reasonably priced.

7) Occasionally splurge. Everyone enjoys the feeling of being able to splurge once in a while. People who live year after year being super frugal and are never generous with themselves are rarely generous with others. Over time, jealousy of others often develops. Such extreme frugality isn't worth it. But be smart with splurging. It is still way cheaper to splurge on a nice lunch or a new outfit than it is to splurge on an expensive watch or a fancy car. Control yourself, and occasionally splurge on the small stuff that matters to you.

8) Find a system that works for you, and then review and make adjustments periodically. There are many ways to manage your finances:

- Separating cash into envelopes for each area that you allocate. When the envelope is empty, your spending in that area is done for the month.

- Budgeting on paper and tracking your spending.

- Using computer software to track your finances.

Which method you use isn't important. It just needs to be one you are comfortable with and follow consistently.

A Word About Those Living From Donations

A priest in the Old Testament or a minister in the New Testament are the only ones God designed to live from donations. That is why many preachers preach about giving and give examples from their own life on how God sent people to bless them.

The other 11 tribes in the Old Testament were supposed to work their land. And the Lord would bless the work of their hand. The predominant way God's blessing comes is by opening up amazing opportunities, and by blessing the work we do as we engage in these opportunities. But we still have a part to play in being prepared to engage in the opportunity

CHAPTER 7

Dreams and Visions

Dreaming

"If you can dream it, you can do it."

-Walt Disney

Leaders are Dreamers

Imagining what the future might be is vital. We cannot intentionally form a future that we have not first imagined. This is why all leaders are dreamers. Leaders go where others have not yet gone; they do what others have not yet done. But before they get there, they sit and dream it. Just like coaches tell athletes all the time, "See yourself do it, see yourself scoring that goal, see yourself win," we also need to envision winning in life.

Remove Limitations

One of the keys to dreaming is ignoring all limitations. Ask yourself questions like, "What would I do in life if money, time, and resources

73

> LEADERS GO WHERE OTHERS HAVE NOT YET GONE; THEY DO WHAT OTHERS HAVE NOT YET DONE. BUT BEFORE THEY GET THERE, THEY SIT AND DREAM IT.

were never an issue?" Or "If nothing is impossible and everything is doable, what would my life look like?" Dreaming involves every area of life. From accomplishments to finances, from family and friends, to housing and vacation. We need to think about all areas and start imagining how things could be.

Often, in childhood and teenage years, we are full of optimism and dream about all kinds of things. We have visions of what we want our future family to be like, what kind of house we would like to live in, how we want to help multitudes of other people, where we want to travel, and how we would like to be a professional hero, maybe as a doctor or a firefighter saving lives. When we are younger, we also often dream outside the boundaries of physics and natural laws. We dream of bullet trains—transportation that can take a person from one continent to another in just a few minutes—or we might dream about settling on a remote planet.

Somewhere along the way, we start looking at limitations, reduce our goals, and live on a smaller scale than what our dreams once were. We become aware of obstacles and limitations and think in terms of what can be done with the time, finances, and energy at hand and within the boundaries of what is possible for ordinary people. The problem is, it is impossible to dream inside this framework and be successful. With limitations in mind, you can at best only dream of what an average person is already doing. But history is full of examples of people who did what others thought was impossible because they dared to dream beyond known limitations. Flying used to be impossible until the Wright brothers refused to limit their dreaming. Traveling to the moon used to be silly thinking until a group of people at NASA dreamed beyond current limitations. People used to think it was humanly impossible to run a marathon in less than two hours, until Eliud Kipchoge did it. Many things are possible, but they all start by someone dreaming beyond what others think are limitations.

Set Aside Quiet Time

In order to dream freely, we need to set aside quiet time. It is difficult to dream while we have all kinds of responsibilities and daily tasks on our minds. Dreaming requires that we quiet all our day-to-day activities and once again start imagining and engaging in limitless daydreaming.

Personally, I spend at least a week, sometimes two, right around Christmas or New Year. It's a time of reflection on what was accomplished that year, what lessons can be learned from mistakes, and dreaming about the future. Sometimes I dream about goals and visions for the coming year. Other times I think about what I would like my future to look like 15 or 25 years down the road. And then of course throughout the year, I set aside days where I relax and dream. On a weekly basis, I take time to plan my schedule for the week. Often I spend Sunday afternoons evaluating how I am doing on long-term plans and setting goals for the upcoming week.

Prayerfully With God

In my quiet time, I don't just engage in casual daydreaming. I also communicate with God. All too many people come up with their own dreams. Then in prayer, they ask God to bless and prosper their plans. Life works so much better when we humble ourselves, get before God, and ask what His dream is for us. Once we get His dream for our lives, then we have something that has already been blessed by the Almighty.

Psalm 37:4 tells us, "Delight yourself in the Lord, and he will give you the desires of your heart." There are two interpretations here. One is that when we delight in and spend time with God, the dreams of our heart will come to pass. The other interpretation is that when we spend time with God, He will mold our heart and place the right dreams in our heart. Both interpretations are correct. When we fellowship with God, He places His dream for us into our heart, so that it becomes our dream. And then He helps make those dreams come to pass. It is an amazing process. As we take joy in worshiping the Lord and spending time in His presence, His purpose for us becomes more real, His dreams are placed within our hearts, and we desire to do His will even more. Then, as we continue with Him, those dreams come to pass. There is no limit to what God can do with someone who is surrendered to Him. He will work in us and through us, and we live the blessed life in the process.

Dream Big

> "The greatest danger for most of us is not that our aim is too high and we miss it, but that it is too low and we reach it."
>
> -Michelangelo

IF YOUR DREAM FOR THE FUTURE IS SOMETHING YOU CAN DO IN YOUR OWN STRENGTH, YOU ARE THINKING TOO SMALL.

On the campus and in the classrooms of Oral Roberts University, we were often reminded of the words, "Make no little plans here." Oral Roberts was a big dreamer, and he wanted us as students to learn the secret of dreaming and planning big. The Bible is full of people who accomplished more than what they could have done in their own limited abilities. Noah had to dream big. Moses had to think big. Joshua had huge shoes to fill. Gideon had to grow his thinking before he could accomplish anything. I often tell my students, "If it is possible to accomplish the dream you have, throw it out, and get the dream that God has for you." Said differently, if your dream for the future is something you can do in your own strength, you are thinking too small. God will only give us life assignments that are so big, they will require reliance on Him to accomplish it.

God wants us to do the impossible. In Mark 9:23, Jesus said, "All things are possible for one who believes." Impossibilities ought to be the breeding ground of dreams for the believer. To the one who knows and trusts God, nothing is impossible. Hebrews 11:6 says, "Without faith it is impossible to please him." A dream that doesn't require faith in God to accomplish isn't much of a dream. Personally, I have lived like this for a while. I can't imagine living any other way. Fellowshipping with God Almighty, dreaming with Him, and then seeing Him work in and through me in order to accomplish dreams and impossibilities is just an awesome and thrilling life.

Write Down Our Dream

In order for dreams to become realities, there is a sequential process it must go through. The process starts by writing down the dream. Studies show you are 42 percent more likely to achieve a goal that you write down.[7] There are lots of ways you can write down your dreams. Some use a vision board placed somewhere they'll see every day. Others carry a note with them everywhere they go. How and where you write it down isn't the most important, but it is important to look at it and think about those dreams on a very regular basis.

I don't journal nearly as much as I should, but I always have my journal with me, ready to jot down ideas as I dream. For years, my journal has contained my dreams. I look at it regularly, and throughout life, I update it. What does not get written down rarely gets done. A dream is no good if it only remains in our head or in our heart.

When you start out, a list of dreams written down might look like this:

- Start a business
- Get into full-time ministry
- Live overseas
- Make lots of money
- Get a better or bigger house
- Go on a dream vacation

It does not need to start off as a long or elaborate list, and it doesn't have to start off very detailed. Write down whatever you have in the beginning. As you spend more time and get used to dreaming, the list will grow, the details will become more defined, and the dreams will often grow in size. Don't despise the small beginnings (Zech. 4:10). Over time, dreams may refine and start looking more like this:

- Own a 3,000 square feet vacation home with a view in Aspen, Colorado
- Spend two years outside Paris, France, with the family, working for INSEAD business school
- Build two homes in the Appalachian mountains for missionaries to come and rest on furlough
- Have a net worth of one million dollars by age 30

This is just a sample. The dream list can get long. And it should get long—30, 50, or even 100 items long.

In January 2015, I spent some time thinking about long-term life goals. I wrote down a list of things I wanted to accomplish in 15 years. The dreams seemed huge at the time. Surely, I would have to walk with God to see any of them come to pass. Then I started doing what I am about to share in the next several pages. I turned the dreams into goals, and started planning and working towards those goals. In only three years, I made so much progress on the 15-year goals that they all seemed too easy to accomplish. I grew personally, and was making great progress on my dreams. So I had to revise my goals and make them much bigger. I realized it was possible to get so much more done in my lifetime than what I imagined.

Dreaming Yet Bigger

Many people make the mistake of dreaming about what only concerns their life. Some do the same in prayer. We humorously quote those who pray, "My name is Jimmy and I'll take all You'll gimme." Or a family who prays, "Bless us four and no more." But there is no such thing as a successful and content person who does not live to be a blessing to others. Many dream of living in a million-dollar mansion, having a beautiful family, driving an exotic sports car, and having the money and time to go on dream vacations. I have no problems with any of those, and believe they are all appropriate. At the same time, if those are at the top of our dream lists, then our thinking is still extremely small and self centered. A God-given dream will always include making lives better for multitudes of other people. Like Zig Ziglar said, "You can have everything in life you want, if you will just help enough other people get what they want." In other words, if you have million-dollar dreams, you better make sure you have dreams that include providing a million dollars in value to other people. Some only earn minimum wage because that is the value of the services they offer. If your own stuff is at the top of your dreams list, start over. Make some adjustments in your attitude and values. Think about being a giver, then dream again.

Dream Often and Dream Much

Do this often. Weekly, monthly, annually. Optimists are dreamers and dreamers are optimists. But make sure you turn the page, and turn your dreams into visions, goals, and plans. And then take action!

Visions or Goals

"A goal is a dream with a deadline."

-Napoleon Hill

A Goal Is Measurable

Once you have dreamed, those dreams need to get refined. When dreams get specific, they become goals. For example, some may dream of starting a business. But that is so vague it is hard to call it a goal you can start working towards. A vision or a goal is something specific. Napoleon Hill, who wrote *Think and Grow Rich* said, "A goal is a dream with a deadline." Someone once said, "When you put a due date on your dream, then you have a goal." I would say that a goal or vision needs to be easily identifiable and measurable.

For example, if you decide to start a business, what does that look like to you? Is it buying a few rugs at a store, and then going door-to-door through neighborhoods selling them? Is that starting a business to you? Some might say yes, but many would not. Or when you consider starting a business, are you thinking of a corporation in a particular industry with corporate offices and a team of employees? Whatever general thoughts you have surrounding your dream, you need to start clarifying and defining them. Be so specific that when another person reads it and looks at your life, they can quickly tell whether you accomplished your dream or not.

Narrow Your List

At some point, you need to go back to your dreams and select a few that are most important to you. If you work on them all, they will all escape you. Few things are as frustrating as a project that got started, but never finished. That is a waste of time, energy, and resources. It is the old principle of not biting off more than you can chew.

Some say pick the top three. Others will say the top five. Whatever number of dreams you pick, make sure they are finite. The trick is to make sure you are not working on the dreams you didn't pick, at least not yet. Once you have accomplished your top dreams, then you can attack some of your other dreams. Remember, a jack of all trades is a master of none. While you can accomplish much, and do many things that seem impossible, you can't do it all.

>>> **ACTION STEP**

PRACTICE DREAMING

Let's take some time to put into practice what you just learned. This book will only help if you actually do what you're reading, so take 15 minutes to dream right now. Grab a blank sheet of paper. If you don't have one, use the inside cover of this book. As you dream, make your list as specific as you can. Once you are done, carefully select the top three to five items on your list. You need to decide what items on your dream list are the highest priority to you. When you have selected your most important, reflect on this question, "What have I done in the last seven days with the items I have decided are most important?"

There's a story about a conversation Warren Buffett, who has a net worth north of $80 billion, had with his pilot. Buffett asked him to list his top 25 career goals. Once his list was complete, he asked the pilot to circle his five most important goals. After lots of thought, he settled on his top five and vowed to work on them right away. The billionaire then asked what his plan was for the other 20. The pilot responded by saying he would work on them as well, but not as hard since they weren't as urgent. And that's when the teaching moment happened.

Buffett told him, "Everything you didn't circle just became your 'avoid-at-all-cost list.' No matter what, these things get no attention from you until you've succeeded with your top five."[8]

A Vision and Drive

If you go look at your dreams, it should be a longer list of things you *could* do. But when you are asked to circle only the top three to five dreams, you need to ask yourself the following questions: "Which of these goals can I not live life without?" and "What items here are so important that if they are not part of my life, then I will never be satisfied?" In other words, vision is what you *must* do, not just what you *could* do.[9]

Apart from vision, you must have the drive to see it come to pass. Without that drive, you won't have the energy to accomplish something big. Your drive is found in those things that you won't be satisfied without. Successful people don't just do what makes them money. They find what they are passionate about and then figure out how to use their passion to help and benefit other people. When you find other people's problems that you are passionate about solving, they will be happy to pay you, and making money will come as a natural byproduct.

A Long-Term View

Working on goals is long term. If your goal can be accomplished in five minutes or two days, you have a goal that anybody can reach, and it will never separate you from average people. A Rolex watch isn't made overnight. It contains high-value metals that went through a long process from raw rock in a mine to a highly refined metal. There are other manufacturing processes involved that have been refined over decades and centuries. These processes were fueled by a drive to always look for a way to make things better and a willingness to continually make improvements. A lot went into making one of the world's most valuable watches.

Valuable dreams do not come to pass overnight. But there is hardly a limit to what can be done in a lifetime if you consistently apply yourself and remain focused on the same goal. If you pick the right three to five items from your dreams, those items will be there every single time you dream. That's what you need to spend some decades and maybe the rest of your life working on.

"Most people overestimate what they can do in one year and underestimate what they can do in 10 years."

-Bill Gates

Planning

"Vision without execution is just hallucination."[10]

-Thomas Edison

Once you have a finite list of specific, measurable goals, you need to start planning. Simply put, a plan is a defined sequence of steps that, when executed, will produce a goal. When you take a larger goal and break it down into individual steps, then you have started planning.

This is one area that will really vary depending on what you want to accomplish. In principle, all planning involves defining steps that are needed to accomplish a goal. But planning to construct a building will look quite different from planning a dream vacation. And both of those will look very different from planning to build a colony to populate the planet Mars.

Similarly, a business plan will be quite different from a building plan.

If you are building a structure, you may need to start with a parcel of land, work with an architect on drawings, find a general contractor, meet with the city for building permits, talk to a banker to set up a construction mortgage, engage the various contractors, and then oversee the entire process to make sure the project stays on schedule, within budget, and that quality of workmanship is up to par.

To start a business, depending on the start-up size, you may need to meet with lawyers to file incorporation papers, work out a marketing plan, set up a system to deliver whatever you are selling, recruit and manage employees, set up financial controls, and so forth.

Whatever you are trying to accomplish, a good plan can help you avoid losses and mistakes and will often help you realize areas you need to learn or grow in. You may need to take some classes, read some books, or talk to others in the field before you can formulate a good plan.

Sometimes step one is to grow personally in a particular area. For example, when I started this book, I was aware that the vast majority of book manuscripts are either never finished or never published. I knew that writing a book can be a significant undertaking and I certainly wasn't interested in starting a project I wouldn't finish. So before I even decided on whether to write this or not, I started reading articles about the writing, publishing, and sales process. Then I talked to several authors about their experiences and asked questions. I needed to have a decent understanding of the size of the project, know what the majors steps were, and then evaluate whether I was willing to commit to finishing a book. Along the way, I found that there are lots of ways to accomplish the various stages. Some authors set aside an hour or two for writing every day. Others will block out two weeks and finish the entire manuscript in that time. There are others who record audio and have it transcribed. When a manuscript is complete, it goes through an editing and design process. Many think the process ends there, but a printed book is useless unless it is sold and read by people.

> WISHING, PRAYING, BELIEVING, AND EXPECTING ARE GOOD, BUT THINGS WILL NOT HAPPEN UNLESS YOU CONSISTENTLY AND PERSISTENTLY KEEP WORKING TOWARDS YOUR GOAL.

So there is research involved that goes into the sales process and decisions to be made on self-publishing versus engaging a publisher. One reason so many projects are never completed is we often don't take the time to think through the entire process before we get started. Anything worth doing is worth doing right.

You need to gain what knowledge you can about the goal or vision you are embarking on, then sit down and create a step-by-step plan on how you will accomplish it. Planning is essential because goals do not automatically come to pass by wishing. They also do not come to pass by praying and believing. Wishing, praying, believing, and expecting are good, but things *will not* happen unless you consistently and persistently keep working towards your goal. No dream is built in a year. That's why you have to be determined and keep making steps each and every day. Even if you don't make huge progress every day, if you will at least do something toward your dream every day, you'll be amazed at how much progress you will make over time.

Planning Systems

There are lots of lots of planning systems available. Here are a few systems or resources you can use:

- The Stephen and Covey Planning System (If you aren't familiar with it, do an Internet search for Franklin Covey Time Management System and you will find links to all kinds of articles, books, and resources.)

- *The Art of Getting Things Done* by Clay Clark

- *Eat That Frog!: 21 Great Ways to Stop Procrastinating and Get More Done in Less Time* by Brian Tracy

Dr. Eugene Swearingen, a well-accomplished businessman from Oklahoma, taught me a very simple planning system I have used for years. I have tried other systems, project management softwares, and smartphone productivity apps. Many of them are good, but for me, I have found that the simpler the system, the more effective it is. Dr. Swearingen's is a very simple pen-and-paper system. He would always carry three cards in his pocket.

- Annual Goals: The first cards contained his goals for the year. Every year, he chose 10 goals for the calendar year and wrote them on a card. One of those goals was how much money he wanted to make for the year.

- Quarterly or Intermediate Goals: Then, he would look at a calendar quarter—the next three months—and decide how far he wanted to get on his goals during that time. He would have a second card, where he wrote his 10 intermediate or quarterly goals.

- Daily To-Do List: Then, each and every day, he would have a new card where he wrote down his to-do list for the day. Some days he would get six items done, other days eight items, and sometimes he would finish his entire list for the day.

Every night, he would mark off what got done, and make another list of 10 items to be worked on the next day. At the end of the calendar quarter, he would update his intermediate goals for the next calendar quarter. At the end of the year, he would evaluate how he did for the year, and plan another 10 goals for next year. The system is brilliantly simple, and I have used a slightly modified version of this for over 15 years. It is so simple, you don't need any education to understand it, yet it was powerful enough to help Dr. Swearingen become hugely influential in Oklahoma.

The most important part isn't the minute details of which planning system to use or even what the specific plan looks like. Don't misunderstand me, the planning step is a critical and important step, but there is more than one way to build a house. At the end of the day, the important thing is that the house gets built. However, the plan does need to be good enough so it can be understood by a team and followed during execution.

Think, but Don't Overthink

If you overthink and overanalyze every detail of your plan, you will never get started. Eventually, you just have to get started. There are times when if you are stuck, it's better to shoot first and aim later. Plan the best you can, keep the big picture in mind, and try to get the first few steps right, because if you don't know exactly what to do, doing something to get started can be the most important.

Emotions, Plans, Dreams, and God

Some things will inevitably change as you plan. Planning forces you to take a vision or dream and think about implementation in light of reality. When you take off limitations during the dreaming phase, you may realize during the planning phase that it is going to require more than you thought. You may realize that you will have to overcome more problems than you initially thought during the dreaming phase. This is normal. You will need to determine whether you are really ready to overcome all these challenges and still pursue your original dream. Or you may need to adjust your dream, maybe let go of a few things, so that you can plan and execute it. There is a bit of give and take between the dream and reality in your planning stage. Faith in God makes impossibilities possible, and it brings reality up to a higher level. How far reality will be brought up to the level of your dream is going to depend on your faith. With true faith in God, there should be some things that are impossible about your dream. But you will still need to determine what you really have faith for, and only go for those dreams and goals that you are really convinced are possible with God's help. If you have the faith, then plan high, bring reality up, and expect God to do great things. If you think your faith isn't where it needs to be, there are a couple of things you can do. One is to get some faith-building materials, study, and then start again. Or you can start with a smaller project and see it through to completion. Both options will help build your faith, and then you start again, but with a bigger goal.

Remember that your dreams, visions, and plans need to be bigger than your emotions. Your emotions will change which could tempt you to change your plans and dreams. God does not change (Mal 3:6), and His callings are without repentance (Rom. 11:29). A true God-given dream will not change next week, next month, or next year. People whose dreams keep changing all the time are not led by God. They are led by their own thinking and emotions.

Build Strong for the Long Term

God's way of fulfilling your dream might not make sense to you or anyone else. I have seen countless people start their own ministry, business, or organization prematurely. Don't forget, Jesus was 30 years old when He started doing ministry. David went through stages—first serving his father, then the king, then a group of society's outcasts— before he led the nation of Israel. Joseph was faithful with his father, with Potiphar, and even in prison before he became the prime minister of Egypt.

In Luke 16:11–12, Jesus said, "If then you have not been faithful in the unrighteous wealth, who will entrust to you the true riches? And if you have not been faithful in that which is another's, who will give you that which is your own?"

So do not be afraid of a plan which seems to take the long road. In life, I would much rather make progress like a tractor which no one can stop, than to try to run like a racecar that spins out at every corner and has no capacity to take anyone or anything with it.

Most of the people I know who accomplished a lot for God experienced what seemed to be detours along the way, which actually gave them knowledge and experience to get through some difficulties later in life. Those who always want to take the shortcut to their end goals often prove they haven't built the faithfulness and discipline to get them through the hard spots in life. Usually, they give up and quit.

In the natural, if you are going to build a huge structure, you need a deep foundation to support it. Similarly, if your goal is big, you may need a deep foundation of knowledge and experience to get where your dreams are taking you.

Personally, I have known since childhood I would be working with people in Africa in ministry. After high school, I went to Bible college and then believed God led me to study engineering. It didn't make any sense to me, but I am very glad I obeyed. While I do not work in the field of engineering today, those studies helped increase my capacity to think, concentrate, and solve problems. Engineering is not about memorizing answers to known problems; it's about creating solutions. As an engineering student, I had many late nights coming up with solutions to intricate problems. I now use those skills daily. I know I would not be where I am today without that knowledge. Many of my friends questioned my decision when I told them I was going into engineering school. It seemed like an unorthodox path, and maybe even a detour. But preparation time is not wasted time. In the long run, it pays to spend time learning and broadening your skills.

Prioritizing

Getting something done means you are saying "No" to a hundred good things you could be doing and only focusing on the great ideas.

When pursuing a big dream, it requires persistence, patience, keeping our focus, and staying the course over the long haul. Focus means that we ignore lots of other tempting affairs in order to get our goals accomplished.

Early on in our work in Africa, we were under severe financial pressure and urgently needed funding. During the wedding reception of one of my wife's friends, I spoke to some pastors of a thriving and growing church. They mentioned wanting to invest into a missions project. Naturally, I became very interested in the conversation. After talking with them a few minutes, I realized they wanted to sponsor some sort of humanitarian missions work—a clean water project, orphanage, hospital, or something along those lines. Those are all great and needed works, but that's not what God called us to do. However, when funding is tight, and funding is offered for that type of work, it was very tempting to add an orphanage or school to what we were already doing. But I knew for us, that would be a distraction from our specific call and mission. So instead of trying to find a way to get a piece of that funding, I referred them to a missionary friend of mine who also happened to be working in Kenya. At the time, he had years of experience getting street boys into a rehabilitation program, and also started schools to educate them so they could become assets to society when they grew up. The pastors at that church ended up working with my friend to build a new primary school in one of the slums of Kisumu, the largest city in Western Kenya.

While I didn't get a single penny from that church, I was extremely grateful I connected them together and played a small part in helping a school for the unfortunate get built in Kisumu. In that case, especially with the financial pressure we were under, it would have been very easy to let that opportunity cause us to drift from what our dream really was. In order for you to accomplish your dream, you do need some financial wisdom, but you surely cannot just follow the money. If you do, you are a slave to money. Money isn't what drives me. I endeavor to walk with God and follow His dream for my life. He will always ensure funding to those who follow His orders.

Find Your Sweet Spot

Prioritizing isn't ignoring things that aren't important. We are all experts at ignoring things that don't matter. Advertisements for feminine products never get my attention, no matter how clever they are. A business opportunity to build a restaurant won't get my attention any time soon, even if there is a lot of money to be made. I am just not interested in feminine products or running a restaurant. But opportunities and distractions in areas that are close to my goals but not exactly on target have strong potential to become distractions. *These are dangerous!* I know all too many people who are working on something in the general direction of their dreams, but aren't quite content. They might be missionaries who have long dreamed of living on the foreign field. Somewhere along the way, they did not refine their dreams to specific, measurable goals. Many knew they wanted to do missions, but never defined exactly what they would specifically do. The dreams were there, but they never defined them well enough so that they became goals. This often resulted in people making it to the missions field, but instead of working on what their dreams really were, they got distracted and settled for working on some project where funding was more easily available. It's painful to watch people who gave up so much with the best intentions, but settled for only living half of their dream.

I compare it to playing tennis. There's a "sweet spot" on the racket that when you hit it, you barely feel the ball make contact with the strings. When you miss the sweet spot, you still make contact, but it's a more jarring feeling. Those are frustrating days on the court. Watching people get close to their dream without fully reaching it is similar. They are still in the vicinity of their dream, but they aren't in the sweet spot. Getting distracted by good ideas that are not really part of your sweet spot dreams just isn't worth it. Don't settle for less than the sweet spot!

Simplify Your Life to Become Great at What Really Matters

There is power in simplicity. The blacksmith who has too many irons in the fire simply won't be effective. He will just be super busy and worn out. There are many times I have declined preaching invitations. I know I need some time for administrative work, and in order to deliver a good message, I also need proper preparation time. If I filled my schedule completely full with preaching appointments, the quality of my messages would suffer. Over time, things would be messy in the office, and the depth of my sermons would be gone. My goal is to deliver high-quality messages every time I speak, and that requires focus and declining some offers, even if they are great opportunities.

Don't Make Every Interruption an Emergency

For the same reason, I have made it a habit of not responding immediately to emergencies. Some fires will simply die on their own without lots of effort to extinguish them. Often, requests for interruptions will go on my scratch pad or to-do list. Whenever I plan my next day or my next week, I may evaluate them to see if they are important enough to become an action item. The problem with important distractions is they take away my time to work on what is *very* important. It is dangerous to work on good ideas and important things. Prioritize and work first on that which is *very* important.

> IT IS DANGEROUS TO WORK ON GOOD IDEAS AND IMPORTANT THINGS. PRIORITIZE AND WORK FIRST ON THAT WHICH IS VERY IMPORTANT.

Prioritize According to What Is Important, Not What Is Enjoyable

Many times, the items that are most important are not those that are not most enjoyable. So, it is always tempting to tackle the enjoyable tasks first, which often doesn't leave enough time for what is less enjoyable but more important. Successful people have learned to control their emotions and desires, and consistently work towards their goals, always tackling the things that are most important and will make the most difference long term.

Control Your Day

To put it simply, prioritizing is all about you controlling life and not allowing life to control you. If you do not prioritize your day before the day gets started, the day will likely control you. Have you ever had something really important that you planned on accomplishing the next day? Usually, the night before you think about your task for tomorrow, then get up a little earlier and get started. By 10 a.m. that day, you are well on your way into your mission, and by noon you may be done. On such an important day, you won't let any kind of distraction derail you. You are determined and the results show! Then think about a day you don't really have a plan. You wake up at a normal time, but by the time you really wake up, finish breakfast, and start thinking about what you will do, half of the morning is gone, and you probably won't have much to show for what you did by lunch time. If you plan each and every day either the evening before or the morning of, you will be far, far ahead of most people. That is why almost all successful people get up a couple of hours before the rest of the world wakes up and start their work before all the distractions of the day start.

Execution

"The fatal flaw in most plans and methods of work is that they are not carried out."

-Terry Lawson in *How to Study the Word*

Once you have dreamed, put together visions and goals, planned them out, and figured out your priorities, you have accomplished a lot. But if you read this book about the process without actually doing it, none of what you're reading will help you. You must get up each and every morning and execute your plans. It takes work to get anywhere in life.

Disciplined Consistency

Have you ever started a project that didn't get finished? I have done it too many times, and each time, all of my labor just went to waste. In one of the houses we owned, we had a lot of unfinished attic space that I worked on turning into an extra room. I put a lot of time and money into that space. I finished the structural changes, put in the subflooring, set the studs for the walls, and did some of the electrical work, but the work was never finished. We never got to use the extra room, and all that work and money never helped the value of the house. Projects like that take time, energy, and money, but it's all wasted if the project isn't finished.

Once you make a decision on a direction, stick to it until you reach the destination. You can't stop and smell every flower along the way or start chasing rabbits. You'll get lost in the woods if you do.

That is why following the system of building long-term goals, breaking them down, and then working on a to-do list every day is critical to reaching any substantial destination. You may get discouraged at how little you can accomplish in one year. But if you are focused and keep working on the same dream, you'll be astounded at how far you go in 10 years.

Have you ever watched a horse race? Believe it or not, we can learn a lesson from these massive animals racing around a track. But our lesson can be found in something that is often overlooked. Each horse wears blinders—small leather squares that block their peripheral vision—so they can only see straight ahead. With blinders in place, the horses won't be distracted by what goes on around them, but rather focus on running towards the goal set for them.

For example, at my house we have a plan for meals and a plan for when we shop. Occasionally, there may be an item missing from the pantry. One ingredient missing from our dinner is not a big enough distraction to keep us from accomplishing what we had planned for the day. So, we just make due with what we have. I'd rather eat a simpler dinner and get something done in life than focus on having an excellent meal every day and that be all there is to life.

Put very simply, you have to get up every day and keep working on what you had planned to do and not allow yourself to get distracted by everything else.

"Discipline is the bridge between goals and accomplishment."

-Jim Rohn

Avoiding Discouragement

Successful people always have a sense of frustration. A visionary will always look at what is ahead and dream about what things should be like. They are not content with where they are and typically wish they were further along at that point in their life. They have a vision for the future and often wish that it wasn't so slow in coming to pass. This is all normal. At the same time, it is important to not let this slight frustration become discouragement. Too much frustration leads to discouragement and can cause someone to give up and become passive. Others are so frustrated by the status quo, that they are always irritable and never happy. Never let the thought of not being far enough along keep you from doing something right now that helps you get towards the goal. There is a balance here. Being content with where we are in life is important. We should be content with what we have. At the same time, we can't be so content that we just passively let life pass us by. The answer is to have a healthy balance. We should enjoy each day, but have enough vision so there is a slight frustration about the status quo that drives us to keep working towards our goals.

I grew up around the ocean, lakes, and mountains, and have hiked a number of mountains. The experience almost always goes something like this: From the base of the mountain, you look at the beautiful view with a sense of vision, excitement, and drive to get to the top. Then you start the hike. Hiking a mountain is rarely difficult, but it requires a good dose of mental perseverance. After you have walked for a while, you keep looking at the mountain and realize that it looks just as big as when you first started. You spend a lot of energy and feel like you are not making much progress. That's when your thoughts start drifting. You might start feeling hungry, wish you were at a restaurant, or maybe wish you went to the ocean instead. If you allow it, those thoughts will discourage you and make you believe that the mountaintop is just too far away. And that discouragement will try to convince you that you are already tired. The more you listen, the more tired you become. But the art of hiking a mountain remains extremely simple. Just put one foot in front of the other. If you focus on that and do it , you will eventually reach the top of the mountain.

The same is true in reaching your goals and seeing your dreams accomplished. You must be relentless in taking small steps toward your goal each and every day.

> "I'm convinced that about half of what separates the successful entrepreneurs from the non-successful ones is pure perseverance."
>
> -Steve Jobs

The Habit of Working on Your Goals Daily

> "If success was determined by great ideas, everyone would be rich; it's about execution."
>
> -Clay Clark

Let's summarize some habits that you can put into place immediately.

- Every day, either early in the morning or the night before, look over your plans and prioritize the five or 10 most important things to be done.

- Put those items on your to-do list for the day and make sure they get done.

Those items should take around six hours to get done. If you put in six solid, effective hours each day working on your dreams and highest priorities, you will surely make progress and eventually reach them. Keep in mind, there will be other things that come up, from packing school lunches for the kids, to interruptions from other employees, or getting urgent calls from vendors and clients. If you only plan about six hours of work that relates to your own goals, you will have time both for family and for other work-related interruptions. If you consistently complete your goals every day, that feeling of accomplishment will be a major motivator that will surely help you keep going.

If you follow the simple steps of dreaming, making specific goals, breaking those goals into planned steps, prioritizing what needs to get done, and focusing on taking action every day, you are guaranteed to advance toward and accomplish your goal.

ACTION STEP

REFLECT OVER WHAT IMPROVEMENTS TO MAKE

Take some time to reflect on this chapter. Ask yourself what changes you need to make in the areas of dreaming, goal setting, planning, prioritizing, and execution. What are some habits you need to do every day? Write down what your new habit of planning is going to be.

Notes

[7] Peter Economy. "This Is the Way You Need to Write Down Your Goals for Faster Success." Inc.com. https://www.inc.com/peter-economy/this-is-way-you-need-to-write-down-your-goals-for-faster-success.html (accessed May 20, 2020).

[8] Mayo Oshin. "Warren Buffett's '3-step' 5/25 Strategy." mayooshin.com. https://mayooshin.com/buffett-5-25-rule/ (accessed May 20, 2020).

[9] Joel Sims: A Leader's Checklist.

[10] Quote is attributed to Thomas Edison, Henry Ford, and many others.

CHAPTER 8

Walking With God

Of all the things you need to get right in life, walking with God is by far the most important thing. Getting to know God is not difficult.

Jesus said, "Come to me, all who labor and are heavy laden, and I will give you rest" (Matt. 11:28). In Peter's first sermon in Acts 2, he proclaimed, "times of refreshing comes from the presence of the Lord." Later in life, Peter wrote, "casting all your anxieties on Him, because He cares for you" (1 Peter 5:7).

Life comes from God. Strength comes from God. Peace and prosperity come from God. All of what really matters in life, including all of our inmost desires, come from God.

Over the years, I have met plenty of people that the world would consider successful. They may have everything and more. In their area of success, I can often learn from them. They might even be an inspiration. But I have never met a person who didn't walk closely with God and seemed fully satisfied with their life.

All of the people I really wanted to imitate have lived in communion with God and regularly saw His mighty hand intervene in the normal course of life. They depend on God to do what is seemingly impossible in life.

I don't know anything more fulfilling, more exciting, and more joyous than to live in constant fellowship with the Creator, continually working with Him so that His desires and plans get executed in the earth. To me, anything below that is just too boring.

In my life, I have walked through all kinds of challenges and problems. In many of life's storms, with circumstances raging (even during the process of writing this book), the peace and contentment within was so strong that the storms often weren't able to affect me. But there were other seasons where life got busy, challenges came, and I spent my time and effort solving the challenges and drifted away from God. It is so easy to try to solve everything in our own strength, and allow the distractions of life to take away from our time with God. When life gets overly complicated, the pressure or the problems are too much, pull back and spend more time seeking God. It is amazing how His presence will first soothe our soul, and when we decide to rely on His strength instead of doing everything ourselves, He has a way or working things out on our behalf.

Listening Skills

True success comes from knowing God and doing His will. In Jesus' earthly life, He gave us an example of how to live. He said, ". . . the Son can do nothing of his own accord, but only what he sees the Father doing" (John 5.19). In other words, Jesus spent time in fellowship with the Father, and then lived in accordance with the instructions He received. When you learn to seek God and develop a close relationship with Him, you'll find that He has a plan and a purpose for you (Jer. 29.11). And He will always guide us, tell us what to do, and show us things to come (John 14:25, 16:13).

It is interesting to note that all of God's instructions through Scripture are simple. Naaman, the leprous Syrian commander, was told to dip seven times in the Jordan river (2 Kings 5). A very simple instruction, yet one that didn't make sense to his natural thinking. But when he chose to fully obey, he was completely healed. The miracle would have never happened unless Naaman was willing to listen and follow the instruction.

At the wedding in Cana in John 2, Mary told the servants, "Do whatever he (Jesus) tells you." Jesus told them to take from the water for washing their hands and take it to the kitchen. Cleanliness was paramount in the Jewish mind, and to take this unclean water to the kitchen made no sense. Yet, when they fully did what they were told and filled the jars to the brim, the miracle of water turned to wine happened.

In John 21, Peter and some of the disciples had been fishing all night without catching anything. Jesus appeared and told them, "Cast the net on the right side of the boat, and you will find some." I have done some fishing in my life. My grandfather was faithfully in his boat almost every morning at 9 o'clock. I know full well that it makes no difference what side you throw the net on. Yet, when Peter did what he was told, they caught 153 fish, more than the net was supposed to be able to hold.

Lots of people don't understand, "Give, and it will be given to you" (Luke 6:38). So they do not obey, and then go without the blessings. Many others don't understand, "Honor your father and mother, . . . that it may go well with you and that you may live long in the land" (Eph. 6:2–3). So they dishonor and pay a heavy price as a result.

WHEN OBEYED AND ACTED UPON, GOD'S INSTRUCTIONS ALWAYS YIELD PHENOMENAL RESULTS.

His instructions are consistently simple. Yet, they are consistently contrary to human thinking. But when obeyed and acted upon, God's instructions always yield phenomenal results.

Story of Nairobi Office

In 2016, Cathrine and I had worked for years in Kenya and set up schools in several towns. Through prayer, we knew that it was time to move to Nairobi, Kenya's capital, and open a campus there. Because of cultural differences and the influence of the city, we also knew that we would have to think differently about a number of things in order to be effective. Nairobi had taken the top spot for cities in Africa to attract multinational companies. Google, Coca-Cola, IBM, and a long list of other companies had all chosen Nairobi as their African hub, and that really impacted the development of the city, both with respect to infrastructure and culture.

In order to be effective, we knew we would need offices and school premises with a much higher standard. We moved our family to the city in August 2016 with the goal of opening a school by September 2017. As we looked at commercial space for rent, learned the real estate environment, and budgeted what the income and expenses of the school would look like, it didn't look easy.

Nairobi is well known for its traffic problems, so we would sometimes use Sundays and public holidays to explore and get to know the city. One holiday in August 2017, as we passed a new commercial building, I knew in my heart that there was something special about the building. We came back during business hours, found an agent, and looked at all the available office spaces. With each floor and each space, something just didn't seem right. It reminded me of the prophet Samuel looking to anoint one of Jesse's sons as the next king, and one by one, the Lord said, "Neither has the Lord chosen this one" (1 Sam. 16:6–10). The price was also far outside our comfort zone. As we left the building that day, we wondered what to do and where to look next. To add to that, time was short. It wasn't easy to be under such time and financial pressure. The "smart thing" to do was lower our standards, set up an agreement with a hotel where we could rent a classroom on an hourly basis, and easily make changes based on how many students actually enrolled. But I knew in my heart there was something that needed to be done at the new commercial building, no matter what the "smart thing" was.

So, we went back. This time, we happened to run into a maintenance employee, who surprisingly knew of another open office that the agent had not told us about. When we walked in, we knew this was it!

Had we not listened and went back, we never would have found it. But we weren't finished with the deal yet, and there was still plenty of pressure trying to draw our minds away from God's instructions. The Bible college was to open in just over a week and we still didn't have enough money for initial rent and the deposit. We talked to the owner, who gave us favor and we negotiated a very good deal. He drafted the agreement and sent it over to us. While I was at peace with the agreement, we still didn't have enough money, and there were only seven days left until school opened. The pressure was on, but I buckled up, spent extra time in prayer, and made sure I kept peace in my heart.

I asked the Lord, "Is there any step You would like me to take?"

I heard, "What would you do if you had the money?"

I would have signed the contract! I knew the Lord wanted me to act in faith and sign the contract, so that is exactly what I did. We were now responsible for rent in a commercial building over the next two years, and we didn't even have the cash for the down payment. Without any solicitation, two days later, a donation came and we completed the deposit and initial rent payments. We had the key to the facilities two days before school opened, and everything started on schedule just like we had announced. Today, we have a beautiful office and classroom in a high-class business district in Nairobi. Listening isn't always comfortable, but the practical steps are easy, and the end result are stories we could not produce in our own strength if we tried.

Warning

Let me warn you about something. Don't just copy the actions that someone else did in obedience to God. Pharaoh's army tried copying Israel's actions of crossing the Red Sea and they drowned (Heb. 11:29). I've seen many people get themselves in a predicament by copying what they've seen others do or by trying to do what God had spoken to someone else. You have to get your own instructions from God and walk with Him yourself.

True Riches

While we strongly believe in having success and finances, we also know that money does not produce happiness. Money is a tool, and money can do things that can help in almost every area of life. Yet, having money is no guarantee for happiness. Far from it.

Similarly, accomplishing something in life is good. We certainly don't want to see anyone going through life and not accomplishing anything meaningful. Everyone ought to be part of making the world a better place and being a positive influence by helping others. Yet, someone can be accomplished and not be happy.

Solomon wrote, "Better is a little with righteousness than great revenues with injustice" (Prov. 16:8), and, "Better is a little with the fear of the Lord than great treasure and trouble with it" (Prov. 15:16).

Proverbs is full of instructions on how to have both money and success. Yet, there is something that is far better. In Luke 16:11, Jesus said, "If then you have not been faithful in the unrighteous wealth, who will entrust to you the true riches?"

What are the "true riches" Jesus mentioned? It's something everyone wants, something far better than the finances and success of this world. I have personally met a number of people who are Christians, make good money, have accomplished things in this world, yet they are not truly satisfied. Like I said earlier in the book, when people hear of what we do, they often say, "That must be rewarding." And they are right. I can't say that everything is easy, but I can truly say that life is rewarding, satisfying, and that I have a peace within that passes all understanding.

Within every person, there is a yearning for inner satisfaction. There is a desire for a peaceful and content life. Neither money, accomplishment, great learning, self discipline, religion, nor pleasure can truly satisfy this deep desire. Solomon tried all of those and wrote, "This is vanity; it is a grievous evil" (Ecc. 6:2).

Peace with God is what every person is yearning for. This peace starts when we believe in the forgiveness offered through Jesus. Romans 5:1 says, "Therefore, since we have been justified by faith, we have peace with God through our Lord Jesus Christ." And Romans 8:1 paints more of the picture, saying, "There is therefore now no condemnation for those who are in Christ Jesus." When we know that our relationship with God is not based on our own works, but rather on accepting what Jesus did for us, we enter into a peace that nothing else in this world can provide.

I know many Christians who start this new life with great joy, eagerness, and peace. But in their walk with God, He will invariably highlight areas in our lives where He calls us to live on a higher level and become more Christlike. Many grow with excitement at first, but over time, very often there are areas where they choose to keep doing things according to their own way and according to their old life. Some carry small grudges against others, some don't want to give up habits, and others don't want to make sacrifices that God asks of them. Over time, not obeying Him leads to a hardening and a conscience that isn't quite clear. That is why many know they have peace with God, but they also know that there must be something more or something deeper available.

True riches only come when we fully follow God, lay down all of our own goals and desires, and wholeheartedly embrace what He has for us. That is when life becomes exciting, full of adventure, yet at the same time full of peace and contentment.

Paul testified of living life with a clear conscience, saying, "I serve God with a clear conscience," (2 Tim. 1:3) and, "I have lived my life before God in all good conscience up to this day" (Acts 23:1). If life were a choice between money, accomplishment, fame, and a clear conscience, you'd better take the peace that comes from a good conscience and let everyone else fight over the rest. The true riches that God gives are just so much better.

If you do not know Jesus or do not have a clear conscience with God, I would encourage you to stop here, turn to page 161 called

"Finding Jesus" in the back of the book and pray the salvation prayer on that page. It will be the best decision you ever make!

Day by Day

Knowing God and walking in peace needs to be a daily habit. There are many approaches and lots of resources available to help. What is most important is to form a solid habit. Here are some foundational recommendations that will help produce a lifetime of rich experiences with God. Though I have walked with God for decades, these are still solid basics to be reminded of.

>> Set a consistent time and place where you can focus.

God is a Spirit, and He speaks to us through our spirit (John 3:6–8; John 4:23; Rom. 8:14–16). In order to fellowship with God, it is important to have a set place and time where there are no interruptions. You need an environment where you can quiet your mind and soul. Personally, my best time is early in the morning while the rest of my family is still asleep. I like starting my day with God, and allowing my time of fellowship to linger with me throughout the rest of the day. Exactly when may not be the most important question, but it does need to be a consistent habit. If you are going to hear from God, you need to learn to shut out mental distractions.

>> Make Bible reading part of your habit.

The Bible is by far the world's best-selling book. It ranks so far higher than anything else, that bestseller lists simply don't consider Bible sales. It is also the most feared book in the world. Many governments have banned its printing and distribution, because they know if people read it, it would change the culture and world view of their nation. There is tremendous power in the Lord's instructions. Reading commentaries and books about the Bible is good, but it can never replace reading the Bible. A good daily dose is the best antidote against the thinking of the world. It will keep you thinking in line with the truth and keep your life on course. There are a couple different ways of reading that are both important and highly recommended. One, for a well-balanced life, make sure you read the Bible systematically or in its entirety. Don't just pick your favorite scriptures, but seek the whole counsel of what was spoken. So many people just read through the colored lenses of their denomination or upbringing, focusing on certain sections of scripture and skipping others. All of Scripture was meant to be read and it is meant to be understood. I would highly recommend picking one of the books of the Bible, and reading the entire book quickly, preferably in one setting. For example, start with the Gospel of John, and read all 21 chapters in one or two sittings. Don't stop to analyze details or ask questions about small sections you don't understand. You want to read quickly and get the overall meaning of the book. Every small detail fits into a bigger picture, but those details will be much harder to understand if you don't have a good handle on the big picture. The second way to read the Bible is also equally important. Read a passage or a chapter, then think over what was said and its meaning. Don't rush, but rather meditate and ponder on God's instructions and how He dealt with people. Most of all, look for how you should apply instructions to your own life. When you combine both these ways of reading Scripture, you will get a better grip on the overall meaning and the big picture, and you will be better able to understand the details and how to apply God's principles in your own life.

If you are still wondering how to get started, then you can find a Bible reading plan. Buy a copy of the One Year Bible or use Bible apps and follow a reading plan. Personally, I read from paper where it is easier to underline, take notes, and there are no digital distractions. Or you can go through the New Testament in one year, simply by reading one chapter per day.

>> Attend a good church with good pastoral input.

There are a number of reasons why regular church attendance is critical. As important as church is, you won't find one that is perfect in every way. If I were to find a perfect church, it would cease to be perfect the moment I joined it. A church is made up of a group of imperfect people. But we need each other. For one, everybody needs to be immersed in a group of strong believers. The fellowship is vital and impacts our emotional health, is a source of spiritual input, and provides opportunities for us to help others. Second, God gave pastors as ministry gifts to help us grow (Eph. 4:8–14). Spiritual father figures whom we listen to for advice, who become examples of stability, and provide care when life is hard are simply needed in a world where most seek their own desires. Find a good local congregation where there is good spiritual nourishment every week and where believers come together having an attitude of giving life unto others. Some argue that all of this can be accomplished outside of a church, but I have never seen anyone with a free-spirit attitude get very far in their life with God. Growth with God only happens as we submit to Him, learn to receive from people who are spiritually endowed as ministers, learn to submit to one another, and not run at the first sign of offense. Church attendance helps us to grow strong through both pastoral input and by building relationships with other believers, and these are pillars that helps us stand through the storms of life.

>> Additional resources (podcasts, books, etc.)

Church is important, but you will not get sufficient spiritual input by listening to a 30-minute message once a week. Your pastors will not be doing all of your spiritual growth for you. He is only a coach helping you on the way. Whatever your preferred mode of learning—reading books, listening to podcasts, watching videos, or attending seminars or small groups—you need to build yourself using additional resources. Just like we all need resources to help us grow in life, professional, and business skills, we also need resources to help us grow in our spiritual development and our life with God. Personally, I grow most by reading. About half of the books I read are on business and leadership, the other half are related to the Bible. Once in a while I supplement a little with general knowledge in various other areas of interest.

>> Daily prayer

Prayer is so much more than just asking God for help. Making our request known for the situations we encounter every day is certainly part of a healthy prayer life, but fellowship with God also includes thanksgiving and worship. The habit of consistently giving thanks to God for what He has done does wonders. It clears your mind of problems and resets your attitudes about life. Everyone can find a problem if they look at their circumstances. But focusing on other things will help fill our hearts with gratitude. If you have a knee or a back hurting, start by being thankful for the parts that are working. If you had a meal to eat in the last 24 hours, you have something to be thankful for. There are a lot of people around the world who went to bed hungry last night and are in worse shape than us. Being thankful to God for what we do have is so much better than always complaining about what we don't have.

If fellowshipping with God, praying, and all this church stuff is new to you, then this is a great way to get started. Thank God that He made a way for you to be alive and that He provided you with shelter and food. And He gave us instructions for how to live, so that we should not go without hope. Thanksgiving places our focus on the goodness of God, takes our eyes off problems, and makes life so much better.

>> Throughout the day

This might be the most important of all. If Bible reading, prayer, and going to church become chores to be ticked off a to-do list, they are no longer effective. Just like you can't go on a date with your spouse with the mentality of ticking the task off your to-do list, so our relationship with God is not a chore to get done. Live each and every day remembering to be grateful for what God has provided for us. Taking moments throughout the day to express our heart to Him will bring us a long way towards living a life of walking with God.

CHAPTER 9

Building Bridges

L ife is short. Compared to eternity, James calls our lives a vapor that passes away (James 4:14). At the end of it all, our possessions and personal accomplishments will not matter much. At a funeral, very few will talk about possessions. Some may talk about accomplishments. Almost everyone will talk about relationships and how we helped each other. The stories of how we connect with others will long outlast any of our material possessions.

We Need Others, Others Need Us

"Iron sharpens iron, and one man sharpens another."

-Proverbs 27:17

Apart from our relationship with God, nothing is more important in life than how we relate with other people. Personally, I am an introvert by nature. I was the engineer that could concentrate for hours on a problem, and thought I could live very well not having to interact with many people. But somewhere along the way, I realized it would be selfish for me to isolate myself, instead of reaching out to build other people, help others where I could, and learn from others where I needed to grow. I am so glad I changed and chose to live a richer life.

THERE IS NO REAL SUCCESS IF OUR LIVES AREN'T FULL OF MEANINGFUL RELATIONSHIPS.

I have seen people who seem to be successful in so many areas, but struggle with relationships. Having a beautiful home and an exotic car will do little good if your home is full of turmoil or loneliness. In fact, there is no real success if our lives aren't full of meaningful relationships. A life filled with stuff or material possessions but void of great comradery is an empty life. Great relationships not only help us emotionally, but are also the avenue through which we help the world.

There is an African proverb that says, "It takes a village to raise a child." No one achieves greatness by going it alone. Someone might be able to build a cabin in the woods by themselves, but in order to build something significant, like the pyramids or the Eiffel tower, it is going to take a team. Likewise, you don't find Olympic gold medalists who journeyed alone. Even athletes competing in individual events have a strong support team around them.

The Generous Mindset

Many people ask themselves how their lives can be filled with great people. The answer is simple. When we build within ourselves qualities that other people want to be around, we'll never have a problem having great people around us. Rev. Mark Hankins said, "Generous people like to hang around generous people." In others words, if our focus is always on what other people can do for us, if we are more "taking-minded" than "giving-minded," we end up hanging around other "taking-minded" people. Said differently, selfish people will only be left with selfish people to hang around, because the generous people eventually get tired of selfish people clinging to them.

Your mouth is attached to your mindset. Gossip and negative talk about others are hallmarks of poverty. Small minds find ways to ridicule the weak and at the same time complain about those who are successful. Keep such poison far away from you.

In all our relationships, it is important to focus on encouraging and building up one another. Complaining and negative talk is toxic (and often contagious) and must be avoided. It has to be gone from your thinking and your talk, and you have to carefully guard yourself that you don't spend time with people who won't stop negative talk.

Eleanor Roosevelt, wife of former United States President Franklin D. Roosevelt, famously said, "Great minds discuss ideas; average minds discuss events; small minds discuss people."

There are many who are able to make a living for themselves. They have grown beyond poverty and are no longer dependent. They will often talk about politics, news, and current events. I grew up in such an environment, and we were taught to be expert debaters about current events. The paradoxical thing was that while we were taught to debate all the ins and outs of various topics, very few of us ever learned how to take action and do something that created and impacted current events. Talk is cheap, and knowledge without action is useless.

Successful people are so busy making progress, they rarely have time to talk about what's in the news. They're aware of current events, but events are rarely important enough to take up time and space in their minds. When they talk about other people, it is usually about their accomplishments and how they were able to overcome difficulties. Those who throw rocks at successful people never end up successful themselves.

> THOSE WHO THROW ROCKS AT SUCCESSFUL PEOPLE NEVER END UP SUCCESSFUL THEMSELVES.

Seek to be an encourager, seek to build others up, and make it a habit to talk about mindsets and actions that lead to success. Leave gossip and news talk alone. That is fodder for those who don't want to grow.

To be successful and live a rich life, we need to both be able to intentionally build the right relationships while we manage conflicts and challenging situations. In the following section, we will discuss how to do just that.

Building Right Relationships

We should approach every relationship with a mindset of benefiting others. Let's look at three important types of relationships we need to intentionally build: relationships with mentors, peers, and mentees.

Mentors

> "Where there is no counsel, the people fall: but in the multitude of counsellors there is safety."
>
> -Proverbs 11:14 (KJV)

Everyone needs someone they can reach out to for advice; someone they can learn from. Call them a coach, a mentor, or an adviser. When I first found out the majority of successful people intentionally develop relationships with a coach or mentor, I was surprised. I thought leaders had it all together. But then I realized that even the world's best basketball players have coaches, even though the player can play the game far better than the coach. That coach is still there to challenge, encourage, develop, and push them further than they would be able to go on their own motivation.

The same is true for all of us. We have certain weaknesses and habits we tend to fall back into unless we have someone to remind and coach us. Those areas need to be dealt with if we want to grow. If we don't have the courage to talk to others about areas where we are weak or need help, we will never get an opportunity to learn and grow.

Moses was strong and led the entire nation of Israel, yet he was also the meekest person on earth (Num. 12:3). He took advice from Jethro, an outsider to the Israelites. A strong person is not one who hides all his weaknesses and pretends they don't exist. Pride will hide and pretend.

Real strength is when we approach weaknesses with humility, yet have the courage to confidently interact with others.

Even in our strong areas, there are opportunities to get better. One who is naturally talented at running will never win any significant races unless they keep practicing to refine what they are good at. There are a lot of preachers who are naturally gifted at preaching. Yet, many could go so much further if they would work on becoming better speakers and ministers. Advisers can help point out the weak spots, encourage us, and instill discipline in areas where we are already good.

How do we practically find an advisor? Start by identifying a number of people who are better than you and start making a list. Many will be happy to help you, some will decline. They may be too busy, they may not be interested in coaching, or they may hit our worst fear by simply sizing us up and deciding they are not interested in us. Don't get stuck trying to analyze why or fall in the pit of feeling rejected. Keep going down your list, and you will get to a yes if you refuse to let rejection stop you.

Before I started writing books, here is what I did. I went online and researched articles about the writing process, the publishing process, and the sales process. Then I made a list of people who had written several books. These were people that either knew me or maybe we had an acquaintance in common. I was looking for people who were a few levels ahead of me, not necessarily *New York Times* bestsellers. Then I would call or email these people and either ask questions over phone or email, or I would ask if we could meet for about 30 minutes to discuss writing.

Now, when you first meet someone, don't start by asking them to commit a lot of time and hope they will take responsibility for your development. They won't. Be respectful of a successful person's time. You need to come up with two or three questions or specific areas where you need advice. Tell them what you want help with and ask if you can have 10 minutes of their time. If your ask is small, most people will be very willing to help. When you meet, make sure it's for the length of time you said it would be. Offer to meet at a place convenient to them. If you will go out of your way to make it easy for them, they will be more willing to help. Many will point you in the right direction and offer advice on books or resources you can use to grow. It's up to you to get those resources and start growing. Report back to them and appreciate their input. If they see that you are willing to make an effort and are taking their advice and growing, they might be willing to offer more. Next time, ask for a cup of coffee or a lunch with them. You may need to take them to a nicer place than you are used to yourself. Again, make it convenient and comfortable for them. This time, you might be able to spend 30 minutes and have a meaningful conversation in an area they are an expert in where you know you need to grow.

If you'll make a habit of asking people who are more advanced than you in various areas and look to implement the advice they give you, it won't be long before you notice that your own thinking patterns have changed and you are growing.

Today, my brother is a captain, flying commercial airlines. He was only 16 when he started taking flight lessons. I remember how he applied himself and spent hours with theory books and in front of Microsoft's Flight Simulator. He really prepared himself well for all of his lessons. When he finished his private's license, he wanted to advance, so he asked one of Tulsa's best flight instructors if he could learn from him. Bill Spratt had flown in World War II, had all kinds of experience from challenging situations in the cockpit, and was known to be a tough instructor. He normally didn't solicit students. His first response to my brother was, "Are you any good? All of my tolerances are only half of what the FAA examiner requires. Are you willing to go for my standard?" During the instrument rating exam, the FAA examiner will require that you fly within +/- 100 feet of the required altitude. Mr. Spratt required that you fly within +/- 50 feet. My brother accepted and learned from the best available. People are often more than willing to help, but only if you show that you really want to grow and that you have the discipline to make some painful choices. As a result, when my brother landed his first commercial job as a first officer, he had better skills and knew more about aircraft than many of his peers. If you apply yourself like this, you will soon have a reputation, and finding mentors won't be hard. In fact, it probably won't be long before someone is asking you to mentor them.

If you show appreciation, treat them with respect, and continually look for something you can also do for them, you may find that you have a long-term relationship. And remember, people that have gone further often have more advanced tastes. Get to know their tastes. If you buy them something, buy from a league higher than yours. If you can't increase the budget for an item, then instead of getting them a shirt you would get yourself, use the same money and buy them some really nice coffee or a high-quality candle.

⫸ ACTION STEP

MAKE A LIST OF POTENTIAL MENTORS
Think through people you know who are doing better than you in various areas where you want to grow. Make a list of five to eight people who you would like to get to know better that you can contact and start asking some questions.

Friends

"Tell me who your friends are and I will tell you who you are."

-Unknown

Everyone needs friends to fellowship with. We choose who we spend time with, and who we choose says a lot about ourselves. The Bible talks about this in Proverbs 27:17, saying, "iron sharpens iron." Our friends will help us become who we are. They shape our thoughts, habits, and attitudes. Just notice how much you think like the friends you already have. Do you have similar jobs? Is your income range the same? Do you share the same values? Are your worldviews and beliefs similar? In order to keep growing it is also important that you surround yourself with friends who are further ahead than you in the areas you want to grow. You may need to spend time with new people. Finding those who will be positive and encourage you is critical to your growth. But remember, you will only attract such people if you are positive yourself. Sometimes you will also have to leave people who are critical or negative in order to grow. This does not mean you become unfriendly with them, but it does mean you cannot spend large amounts of time with them. While we change, our friends typically do not. Therefore, it is important that you have friends who will grow with you.

Mentees

Last, never forget that we were not born at the top of a mountain. When you start making progress in life, make sure you are willing to help others who have not made it as far but are willing to grow. Make sure you don't get so high minded and proud that you can't relate any more to those who have not reached as far. The Bible is full of advice on helping the poor. Solomon wrote, "Whoever mocks the poor shows contempt for their Maker; whoever gloats over disaster will not go unpunished" (Prov. 17:5 NIV) and, "Whoever is kind to the poor lends to the Lord, and he will reward them for what they have done" (Prov. 19:17 NIV).

Our personal journey up the mountain of success and accomplishment can be a great journey. Along the way, there are hindrances and problems that must be solved and overcome in order to reach ever-higher altitudes. But along the road, there are many who are only in it for their own benefit. It can at times be lonely, and it can be disheartening to see many others who are fighting for themselves. Reach down, find a few other people who also want to grow, and bring them with you. Help them. You'll be a real leader, and you'll also reach the top with the satisfaction of having helped some other people along with you.

Difficult Relationships

Where there are people there will be conflicts. Even when we grow and look to be a positive influence in all of our relationships, we will still run into situations where there is friction. Jesus Himself went about doing good everywhere, yet sometimes He got chased out of town, and at other times He had to crack the whip. If Jesus had to walk through relationship challenges, don't expect to be able to live life without any type of conflicts.

The answer to difficulties does not lie in avoiding people and shrinking back. The answer is to manage those relationships well.

The first place I worked when I was 17, one of my bosses was a thorn in my side. Honestly, he wasn't a good manager. But I was young and didn't know how to handle difficult relationships, so I quit, and started working for another company, just to find out they had employees who weren't that easy to work with. Soon I realized that regardless of what company I was in, someone was going to be my least favorite person there. Instead of thinking negatively about these relationships, I slowly adopted the attitude of learning how to better get along with them. Over time, I realized that investing and sowing into relationships that were difficult at the time have reaped multiplied benefits years down the road. Not only is life richer when I am better at getting along with people, but many of the ones I decided to learn to get along with have later become a connection to other great relationships or they have later become a key person to financial blessings in my life.

Don't Sweat the Small Stuff

One of the important lessons to learn is to not let stuff bother you easily. It has been said that a train cannot stop for every dog that barks. Lots of little things that come up in life will simply die if we do not fuel the fire. My grandfather always told us that if you fight with a dirty person, even if you win, you will end up dirty. In other words, fights usually are not worth the cost to engage in.

"A soft answer turns away wrath, but a harsh word stirs up anger."

-Proverbs 15:1

Usually, it is our emotions that want to respond. Either, we want to get angry, or we want to shut down and give the silent treatment. Or worse, we may feel like retaliating.

Some of us need to count to 10 to let those emotions settle. Others may need to sleep on it until the next day. Once the emotions are out of the way, it will be easy to see that a response isn't necessary. In the few cases where a response is needed, you'll be able to handle it with so much more maturity when you think clearly and not with adrenaline and emotions going at the same time.

When conflict arises or you get criticized, don't panic, but do take a hard look at yourself and analyze what you may have done to cause the other party to react. If there is something that could have been avoided or maybe you could have done better, use the opportunity to learn and grow.

Often criticism can be diffused by talking with the person in private. Start by affirming what you agree on, try to listen and understand the other person's viewpoint, then softly explain your position or perspective. Always seek to leave as friends, even if you do not agree 100 percent on the issue. Never accuse or attack the other party. Trying to deal with their personality or attitude seldom works. Just deal with the actual words that were spoken or the behavior as any neutral third party would observe it. When you communicate with the other party, use a higher form of communication than what was used to start the issue. For example, if the problem started in writing, pick up the phone and call. If there was some gossip or something verbal floating out there somewhere, invite the other person to coffee or lunch. This alone will often diffuse the situation.

Never, Ever Burn A Bridge

We all know someone we don't really like. We think our lives would be easier without them. Some have burned bridges with such people. Others have written them off and, in their mind, decided they will have nothing to do with them ever again. Never decide you won't have anything to do with anyone. It is a selfish thing to do.

Yes, there definitely are people who are toxic and need to be kept at a distance, but you never know when the love of God will reach them. They may repent. They may grow. Paul wrote to Philemon about accepting back a former slave who had stolen and cheated (Philemon 1: 10–11). He then found God, repented, and became useful to both Paul and Philemon. Early in Paul's ministry, he wanted to write off John Mark who left Paul and Barnabas prematurely in the middle of their first missionary journey (Acts 15:38). Paul wanted to discard young John Mark, but Barnabas took him under his wing and encouraged him. Towards the end of Paul's life, Paul appreciated John Mark and asked for his help (2 Tim. 4:11). Be an encourager like Barnabas, and never be quick to give up on others.

In my own life, I have been surprised a good number of times from difficult relationships that would have been easy to write off. But instead, I chose to walk in Christlike love and worked hard to keep the relationships. Years later, a number of them have given me recommendations and referrals, and some have even supported our ministry financially.

Reach Out to Restore

If you see your enemy hungry, go buy him lunch; if he's thirsty, bring him a drink. Your generosity will surprise him with goodness, and God will look after you.

-Proverbs 25:21–22 MSG

Restored relationships are so much better than broken ones. Sometimes Christians are really good at following the law—not cheating, stealing, or lying. I don't know how many times I have heard a believer say, "I have forgiven them, but we don't talk anymore." Christ's example is so much higher than that. He forgave and died for us while we were yet sinners (Rom. 5:8). Then He encouraged us to love each other like He loved us (John 13:34).

In one of the stories told by Jesus, He referred to us coming to God to pray or offer a sacrifice. He said, "So if you are offering your gift at the altar and there remember that your brother has something against you, leave your gift there before the altar and go. First be reconciled to your brother, and then come and offer your gift" (Matt. 5:23–24).

Many, including myself, have often thought that verse refers to us having an issue with someone else. In that case, we should reconcile with them. But Jesus refers to a much higher standard. If someone we know has an issue against us, we should be the mature one to reach out and initiate the reconciliation. The one who reaches out first is almost always the more mature one.

Someone once said that to harbor a grudge is like drinking poison and hoping the other person will die. Carrying grudges and harboring ill will against others affects our health, our emotional life, and our reputation. It just isn't worth it. Being the one to initiate and reach out isn't always easy, but remember, winners don't pick the path of least resistance and look for the easy way out.

>>> **ACTION STEP**

REACH OUT TO THREE LONG-LOST RELATIONSHIPS

Take a moment and think of a few friends or family you have not had contact with in a long time. Also think of at least one or two people whom you no longer have the best relationship with. As long as the people aren't dangerous, reach out to them, reinitiate contact, and do something simple and positive for them, whether it is some kind words in a phone conversation, sending them a card, or inviting them to a cup of tea.

Lean Into the Hard Conversations

In life, I see so many that continually avoid conflict. There is nothing wrong with differences of opinion between people. Two that are walking together, whether in marriage, on a church team, or as business partners are going to have some differences of opinions. Whenever you see two people that agree 100 percent on everything, you know you have a leader with a follower who doesn't do any thinking of their own. So conflict is not inherently bad. It just needs to be resolved correctly.

Over time, if you continually avoid conflict, you will have shallow relationships, unnecessarily going different paths, or you will end up suppressing your own creativity. Worse, you may end up harboring bad feelings and putting a lid on things for so long that you eventually explode. Those are not good outcomes. That is why when opinions differ, it is important to take courage and respectfully talk about those differences.

STRONG TEAMS ARE BUILT BY GOING THROUGH DIFFICULTIES TOGETHER.

If you have an employee that is going off course slightly, make sure you coach, correct, and encourage them before they are so far off they need to be fired. I have seen far too many who ended up with a severed relationship because no one had the maturity to talk about things while they could still be resolved. Remember, strong teams are built by going through difficulties together.

When you have a hard conversation, never attack the person or talk down to them. You must seek to encourage and respect them without hiding or downplaying the importance of the issues. If you go into the situation truly valuing the other person with the goal of finding common ground and a solution that will work for all parties, you have a greater chance of building a solid long-term relationship.

Learning to ignore all the non-essential issues while at the same time taking courage to resolve and work out the important issues requires wisdom. It may take some practice to learn the difference, but the benefit of learning this crucial balance is well worth the effort.

Build Solid Relationships and Manage Well the Challenges

Good people skills are crucial to living well. Like King Solomon wrote, "Better is a dinner of herbs where love is than a fattened ox and hatred with it" (Prov. 15:17). In other words, harmonious relationships with little is better than difficult relationships with much. Harmonious relationships are simply worth more than money. Building great relationships starts with having a genuine care for others. The work it takes to intentionally engage mentors, grow together with peers, and help others grow, all while managing challenges is well worth the effort.

Remember, your reputation at the end of your life will be based more on your people skills than your accomplishments and possessions. And the way you respond in situations when emotions are high will build or hurt that reputation. Choosing the high road every time might be the hard way to go in the moment, but you will never regret the long lasting outcomes.

Personally, this is an area I have spent time studying and growing in. I am still growing, but it brings great peace to be able to say I don't have anyone I consider an enemy and there are no people I carry ill will against. I intend to keep it that way, and you can too.

CHAPTER 10

Continual Growth

Do Hard Stuff

The only way to climb a mountain is to keep on walking in the direction it is the hardest to walk—uphill. A life of growth is a life with the habit of always making improvements, never one that always chooses the path of least resistance.

Every day is full of choices. Faced with a long to-do list, it is always tempting to start with the easier things. Completing something simple gives a small boost of satisfaction, but will leave the larger important items undone. No one looks forward to hard conversations, but life does not move forward unless we deal with the areas where we are stuck. At the end of a long day, it may be tempting to watch TV instead of reading a book. Or at a restaurant for lunch, it may be tempting to eat a delicious meal that might put you in an afternoon slump instead of going for something lighter and healthier that gives the energy to produce through the afternoon.

Growing is uncomfortable. The alternative is to take the easy way out now, and later pay the huge price of lost opportunities and harvests that never produced. Poverty is expensive, painful, and full of regret in the end.

I have been involved in education almost my entire life, either as a student or as an instructor. We have probably all seen that some teachers are good at challenging their students and helping them grow, while others are easier on their students and don't set the bar too high. While we are in school, many look forward to the easy classes and dread the harder instructors. Then when we are done with school, we often realize it was the harder ones who helped us learn the most. The ones who allowed us to coast were enjoyable at the moment, but they didn't really help us much. During my high school and college years, I observed that often the distribution of grades was very similar in the easy and the hard classes. Students who made good grades would make good grades in easy and hard classes. Students with poor grades would often get poor grades whether the class was easy or hard. And those in the middle always seemed to stay in the middle. That is because most people have a particular expectation of themselves and will perform according to their own internal standard. If they have an inward standard of always delivering excellence, they will deliver excellence no matter what is asked of them. Those who always cut corners will cut corners whether the job is easy or hard. Very often, the way you wipe down your kitchen counter at home will be the same way you deliver a presentation in the boardroom.

VERY OFTEN, THE WAY YOU WIPE DOWN YOUR KITCHEN COUNTER AT HOME WILL BE THE SAME WAY YOU DELIVER A PRESENTATION IN THE BOARDROOM.

The good news is we have seen many who have gone through the material in this book and made personal inward adjustments—adjustments that over time caused them to start rising and living better lives.

Writing to the Galatians, Paul explained that the desires of the flesh and the desires of the spirit are against one another. The desires of the flesh are those of the fallen human nature, such as strife, anger, drunkenness, orgies and "things like these" (Gal. 5:21). God's way of doing life, which is called the fruit of the Spirit, includes love, joy, peace, kindness, self-control, and so forth.

Paul added, "Do not be deceived: God is not mocked, for whatever one sows, that will he also reap. For the one who sows to his own flesh will from the flesh reap corruption, but the one who sows to the Spirit will from the Spirit reap eternal life. And let us not grow weary of doing good, for in due season we will reap, if we do not give up" (Gal. 6:7–9).

There was a time when I always wondered *How come others seem to get ahead in life? Why is this one so well off financially? Or why is this other person stuck in a position and never getting ahead?* After having studied both the Bible and other books on business and personal development, it has become very easy to see that there is always a reason why a person is where they are in life. Looking at the lives of other people around us—those who have made it further, those who are about where we are, and those who haven't made it very far—it usually doesn't take long at all to identify where they are and why. The level of success you achieve is always in proportion to the risk you are willing to take and the sacrifices you are willing to make. So many have areas of weakness they never do anything about. Sometimes it is fear of the unknown that keeps them from stepping out. It may be a problem with unforgiveness that keeps holding them back. It may be the habit of always wanting instant gratification. Or they may have talents that they never develop. Whatever the case, we always are where we are for a reason. God gave us the instructions for living a good life, and it is up to us to receive that instruction with meekness and live in accordance with Him.

Coasting Is Shrinking

There is hardly such a thing as staying on the same level. We are either growing or shrinking. Once you take the foot off the gas pedal, the car may seem to run at the same speed for a short while, but it won't be long before you notice your speed is dropping. Coasting is shrinking.

Ask anyone who follows a regular exercise program. Maybe it is working out at the gym three days a week. Personally, I run two miles (three km) twice a week and have done this for years. Running is far from my favorite way of working out, but with my travel schedule, I can't join a sports team, and running doesn't require any equipment apart from shoes. I carry them with me as I travel so I can get some exercise. For a long time, I intended to keep a more rigorous gym schedule, but never kept it longer than the typical few weeks a New Year's resolution lasts. Sometimes committing to smaller improvements and sticking to it is better than making huge promises to yourself that you end up not keeping. But even at my low level of exercise, occasionally my travel prevents me from running for a couple of weeks. Only two weeks of coasting is more than enough to notice a remarkable decrease in my stamina. The same is true in all areas of life. What isn't maintained will be lost. When you grow, make sure you don't fall back into old habits. That is why I am a firm believer that the most important habit you can make is the habit of always making small improvements to your habits.

In Proverbs 11:26, Solomon shared a truth we seldom hear about today, "The people curse him who holds back grain, but a blessing is on the head of him who sells it." He followed that up in Proverbs 12:11 when he said, "Whoever works his land will have plenty of bread, but he who follows worthless pursuits lacks sense." In many areas of East Africa, I have observed a lot of land that is barren. Even in areas that have plenty of rain, I have seen land owners go hungry. It isn't alright to have an economic opportunity and not take it, but instead choose to sit on the couch and relax. Every economic opportunity requires that we take some action and work to produce what the opportunity makes available to us.

I have seen those who don't have enough sit idle and allow opportunities pass them by. Poverty is the result. But what grieves me even more is to see that when people have reached where they have enough for themselves and their children, they often relax, coast, and remain on the level of just having enough to feed their own family. While this is certainly better than being poor, it grieves me when people don't understand that an economic opportunity is an opportunity to help other people. Sitting on the couch once someone has enough for themselves is selfish. When you work the land and produce beyond what you need, you are reaching the place where you provide employment for other people. That helps to feed those who are willing to work but are not ready to run their own business. And the grain you produce can be sold, and it will be a blessing to willing buyers. It is a curse to hold back on economic opportunities, but the person who works the opportunity will be blessed. I am not referring to opportunities of taking advantage of the poor or using dishonest scales (Prov. 11:1; 22:16). But the world is full of opportunities that will bless the one who works it, the people they employ in the process, and the customers you provide goods and services to. Making the world a better place means that we don't coast, but we work these opportunities.

Workaholic Dangers

What good is it if your whole life, you put so much pressure on yourself trying to reach for your goals, that you never enjoy the process. All too many have a dream of enjoying life when they get to retirement. That is no way to live. If we can't enjoy the journey, then we are left with nothing but toil and struggle. Some toil and struggle while they are poor. Others toil and struggle all their life while they chase the wind.

In 1963, Heinrich Böll wrote a story to illustrate the conflict between a busy productive life of toil and a simple life of poverty and enjoyment. The story has been changed, adapted and widely circulated over the years and is often referred to as "The Mexican Fisherman and the American Investment Banker."

An American consultant was at the pier of a small coastal Mexican village when a small boat with just one fisherman docked. Inside the small boat were several large yellowfin tuna. The American complimented the Mexican on the quality of his fish and asked how long it took to catch them.

The Mexican replied, "Only a little while."

The American then asked why he didn't stay out longer and catch more fish.

The Mexican said he had enough to support his family's immediate needs.

The American asked, "But what do you do with the rest of your time?"

The Mexican fisherman said, "I sleep late, fish a little, play with my children, take a siesta with my wife, Maria, stroll into the village each evening where I sip wine and play guitar with my amigos. I have a full and busy life, Señor."

The American scoffed, "I am a Harvard graduate and could help you. You should spend more time fishing and with the proceeds, buy a bigger boat. With the proceeds from the bigger boat you could buy several boats. Eventually you would have a fleet of fishing boats. Instead of selling your catch to a middleman, you would sell directly to the processor, eventually opening your own cannery. You would control the product, processing, and distribution. You would need to leave this small coastal fishing village and move to Mexico City, then LA and eventually NYC where you will run your expanding enterprise."

The Mexican fisherman asked, "But, Señor, how long will this all take?"

To which the American replied, "15 to 20 years."

"But what then, Señor?"

The American laughed and said, "That's the best part. When the time is right you would announce an IPO and sell your company stock to the public and become very rich. You would make millions."

"Millions, Señor? Then what?"

The American said, "Then you would retire. Move to a small coastal fishing village where you would sleep late, fish a little, play with your kids, take a siesta with your wife, stroll to the village in the evenings where you could sip wine and play your guitar with your amigos."

That is just a humorous illustration about unnecessary toil. There is a balance between living for enjoyment day after day and living for money. Some of the best advice I ever heard was, "Find something to enjoy each and every day. If that is a coffee at your favorite coffee shop, great. Make sure you shut off distractions, and enjoy that hour. Bring a friend along and enjoy. Or if you enjoy taking a walk in the park or the forest, great. Make it an enjoyable habit. If this is hard to do, you just might be too close to being a workaholic."

Remember, it is the blessing of the Lord that makes rich, and He adds no sorrow with it (Prov. 10:22).

Risk, Comfort, Excuses, and Action

As we make choices in life, there is always a trade-off between comfort and risk. The easy way—staying with what we know— is usually more comfortable, but comes with limited growth opportunities.

More often than not, when you are faced with a choice in life, and one path involves risk and the other leads to the known and comfort, choose the risk. Nursing homes and graveyards are filled with those who wished they would have taken more risk in life. In fact, 39 percent of Americans regret not following their dreams and over 35 percent wish they would have taken more risks in life.[11]

Human tendency is to choose the known, the comfort, or the same as our friends and neighbors. But no one ever won a gold medal by doing the same thing everyone else did. If you are going to be successful in life, you can't just copy what everyone else is doing. You have to be unique and different, and that always requires risk.

Some Make Excuses, Others Take Action

I know plenty of people who are not pursuing their dreams, thinking they have good reasons not to. Some say they are raising a family instead of following God. I would hate to show my kids by example that there is no need to follow God. Others see how successful people work hard and say, "I don't want to get up that early," or "I don't want to work that hard." Well, if that's your mindset, you may have to forgo your dream. I've heard others say, "That's above my pay scale." Well, if you want to raise your pay scale, you'll have to start producing on a higher level. I have been on plenty of nine-hour flights where I am working on a sermon while most everyone else is watching movies. The small seat and cramped leg space in the back of the plane wasn't a comfortable workspace, but I refused to make that an excuse for not making progress. Many times, we traveled to churches ministering and my entire family, all six of us, stayed in one bedroom. After driving all day and when the kids finally fell asleep, I would go into the bathroom to pray and finish my sermon for the next day. I never wanted to speak to the people in the pews without having a fresh word from heaven. It would have been much easier to just go to sleep after a long day, but I would still press in and make sure I had something of quality to deliver.

It doesn't matter what field or profession you look into, the people who made the biggest impact always worked hard, refused to make excuses during the hard days, and kept charging ahead in order to make a larger impact on more people.

Enjoy the Journey

Once you learn how to keep your focus and make progress towards your goals every day, don't do what I did and forget to enjoy the process. Don't make the mistake of continually thinking *When I reach my next goal, I will enjoy life more.* As long as you have vision, there will always be a new and bigger goal ahead. Life is a process and success is a journey. Success is not reaching the end, it's the process of making

SUCCESS IS NOT REACHING THE END, IT'S THE PROCESS OF MAKING PROGRESS.

progress. Make sure you find something to enjoy every day. And once in a while stop, go on vacation, and smell the flowers.

After my sophomore year at Oral Roberts University, I had an opportunity for a summer internship working on some space rocket research that NASA was sponsoring. I enjoyed the challenge tremendously, and was doing so well in school that I had an opportunity to complete my junior and senior years in one year. Something on the inside told me to hold off, but I had my eyes too fixed on the accolade of finishing early with a bang. So I took a very heavy course load of 27 credit hours with some of the most challenging courses the university had to offer. In addition, I did a massive senior design project. I was chasing after success and trying to do too much in too short of time. I finished well, but got exhausted and burned out in the process. It took me several years to recover and get my stamina back.

It took me a while to learn, but now I am better at taking a little time every day to relax and enjoy. For years, it seemed like there never was any time in the schedule for vacation. Then I realized that work was always going to be there. Now, when we plan our schedule for the year, I always write in vacation first, then fill in work around it. Start planning with the most important stuff. Vacation was never happening for us, so we made that the most important part of our annual schedule. Every year, it means there are ministry events we could and maybe should have attended, but spending time with my family on vacation is more important.

Until I made that adjustment, I was in the ditch of never having enough time for vacation. But most people are in the opposite ditch of always looking to have pleasure now and enjoy life. They will have to learn to make goals and prioritize where they want to go.

But when you start focusing on goals, you will get busy. Don't get into the other ditch of being too busy for family and fun. Make those a priority as well. Every day, make sure you get the top priorities done, and then enjoy your day. There will always be more stuff that could have gotten done.

Notes

[11] Jeff Faust. "One-Third of Americans Regret Major Life Choices, But Many Embrace Newfound Opportunity to 'Rechart' Course." Business Wire. https://www.businesswire.com/news/home/20160523005192/en/One-Third-Americans-Regret-Major-Life-Choices-Embrace (accessed May 20, 2020).

CHAPTER 11

Embracing the Whole Picture

The Doctor With the Billing Mess

You don't have to be an expert at everything in life in order to be a success. In fact, being an expert means you are far ahead of the average in a limited area, and that's fine. Those who try to be an expert at everything tend to end up a master of none. Yet, there is a range of life skills we need at least a basic proficiency in. If we are severely deficient in these areas, it will hinder us.

For example, once I was looking for a primary care physician in Tulsa, Oklahoma. After having moved from Norway, it just didn't make sense to refer to a primary doctor thousands of miles away. After returning from one of my trips to Kenya, I had a small wound that had gotten infected, so I went to see one of the doctors in town who had a very high reputation. The doctor visit itself was fine, but there were some issues with the bill afterward. After multiple phone calls with the doctor's billing office, I realized the entire business side of the doctor's practice was unorganized and messy. I kept being sent from person to person. It took such an effort to get things resolved that I finally decided to pay the higher bill and not return to that doctor. He could keep improving his medical skills and go from being one of the best in the city to becoming one of the best in the state, but the business side of his practice was so far below average that I never wanted to be seen by him again.

Many recommend that we become an expert in an area where we are strong. There is some truth to that thought, but that doesn't mean we neglect all the areas where we are weak. Our weak areas are often areas that are important for our success, but they are areas we don't like to improve because it simply isn't enjoyable to keep practicing in an area where we feel like we fail.

But in soccer, having the best ball control in the world will do little good if we don't know how to get along on a team. Any coach would instruct such a player to improve their weak spots and at least bring them to average before they would be able to really benefit from their strong areas.

The Life of David

Early on in the book, we mentioned King David as a figure that gave us a good example of a successful life. His life wasn't perfect, but he grew everything around him, was blessed in practically everything he did, and left a tremendous legacy that has continued to inspire millions for 3,000 years. From his life, we can see that David pursued excellence in a good number of areas, and that balance was part of what contributed to his success.

We first find David in 1 Samuel 16 when King Saul had made some terrible mistakes and the prophet Samuel came to the house of Jesse to anoint Israel's next king. Samuel at that time was probably the dearest figure in the entire nation, and he was coming to Jesse's house. Jesse called his family together. There had to be a lot of excitement that they were going to have a large family party with the biggest name in the land.

Interestingly, David was never invited to the family party, but was instead left to shepherd his father's sheep. Shepherding sheep was considered a low job in the nation, something that his brothers later made fun of him for (1 Sam. 17:28). Yet, despite not being invited to the party, David kept serving his father with excellence. He had an opportunity to carry a grudge against his family. But we know that he served above the call of duty. When lions or bears came to take the sheep, David defended his father's sheep, risked his own life, and took care of the threat.

David also played his harp, worshiping the Lord, and became so good at it, that when the king needed someone to play, David was called and changed the atmosphere for the king with his music. People of success often make a habit of doing everything with excellence. You never know where the next opportunity will come from, but when you do everything with excellence, you certainly have a better chance of getting the next opportunity compared to someone who simply does his hobby haphazardly or casually. Excellence is something others are attracted to and it leads to success.

When David delivered food to the battle lines, he found the entire army of Israel afraid of Goliath. Here, we notice a distinct difference in David's thinking and the thinking of the rest of the army, including his brothers. Those in the army could describe Goliath and knew his height and the details of his weapons. They also knew that whoever could defeat the giant would get a great reward, be given the king's daughter, and become tax free (1 Sam. 17:4–7, 25). Surely, the giant must have been a fearsome sight to behold, standing more than nine feet tall, but when David inquired, he wanted to hear the rewards repeated to him. And then he added, "For who is this uncircumcised Philistine, that he should defy the armies of the living God?" (1 Sam. 17:26). Instead of talking about how intimidating Goliath was, David labeled him as uncircumcised, which meant Goliath didn't have a covenant with God. And instead of being afraid and hiding, David reminded everyone, including himself, that Israel was considered "the armies of the living God." David walked into a dangerous situation, but kept his mind fully aware of who had a covenant with God and who didn't. Such a response never comes from spending time on social media or watching the news. Only those who spend time thinking and meditating on their relationship with God will respond like this in a difficult situation.

David's words and thinking were so different from those around him that he was reported to King Saul and got an immediate audience with him. David never backed down, but continued to proclaim how the giant would be defeated, telling the king, "Let no man's heart fail because of him. Your servant will go and fight with this Philistine" (1 Sam. 17:32). People who are convinced of victory always talk and act noticeably differently from those who aren't sure. Saul pressed David and tried to convince him that he couldn't do it. Another characteristic of those who walk by true faith is that they do not give up or change their mind just because they meet a little opposition and a few arguments against their case. Instead, David told the king, "Your servant has struck down both lions and bears, and this uncircumcised Philistine shall be like one of them, for he has defied the armies of the living God." He continued, "The Lord who delivered me from the paw of the lion and from the paw of the bear will deliver me from the hand of this Philistine" (1 Sam. 17:36–37).

Some great lessons are found here. First, David started serving his father with excellence. He went above and beyond the call of duty back when he was neglected by his family, and stretched beyond expectations when no one was looking at what he was doing. Excellence never starts at the top of the mountain. Excellence in what we do starts when we are washing the floors. If we can't do a small job with excellence, we will also show neglect in weightier matters. Whatever our hand finds to do, we need to make sure it is done right. As we continue exceeding expectations, eventually we will be noticed, given larger responsibilities, and better pay.

> EXCELLENCE NEVER STARTS AT THE TOP OF THE MOUNTAIN.

Second, David relied on the Lord when challenges came. He explained how it was the Lord who delivered him from the lion and the bear. Those who dream of things they can do in their own strength are thinking small. The Lord will always call us to do things that are too big for us, tasks that require reliance and dependence on Him.

Third, David stayed mindful of the things of God and the blessings of God in the midst of adversity. He didn't deny that Goliath was a challenge. He knew the giant was a major challenge just by his massive size. But he had faith and knew God would give him the victory, so instead of running from his challenge, he ran toward it. He reminded himself that Goliath was uncircumcised. David knew he had a covenant with God and probably thought back to the times he spent communicating with God and worshipping Him while he was shepherding his father's sheep. Those habits paid off when he needed it most because those habits held stronger than the voice of the giant and all those around him that told him he couldn't face the giant. These habits must always be stronger than the voices of opposition, and they can only be developed by habitually thinking about them.

Fourth, when others doubted David, he reminded both Saul and himself of past victories with the lions and bears. Facing a major giant is going to be hard if we are cowards in the smaller battles of life. Sometimes resilience and persistence is built by fighting the smaller battles; those we easily could have made excuses for and opted not to face.

Lastly, David ran towards the giant. The closer to a problem you get, the larger it will look. But David never backed down. Instead, he trusted in God and conquered yet another battle on his road of success.

Focus on Strength, but Mitigate Weaknesses

When I walk into a person's house or office, I have a strong tendency to look at the titles in the libraries. Over the years, I have noticed a common trend. I found most people read and grow stronger in areas where they are already strong.

As recently as yesterday, I came across a list of recommended book readings from a group of ministers. I quickly noticed that virtually all of the books they recommended were in the area of practical theology. Lots of great books were recommended. The list was from a group of pastors, and they know well that most theoretical theology does not help the average person. But I also happen to know the group well enough that I know many of them are struggling with growing their churches. I noticed a marked absence of some good business books. I saw very little, if anything, about good customer service, how to manage employees, how to delegate, financial stewardship for businesses, and the like.

So many people I know would do so much better in life if they would just be willing to find out what their weak areas are, then do something to grow in those areas. If you just aren't good with numbers, that's fine. You don't have to grow to be an expert accountant or financial adviser, but you will have to grow in that area enough that you can hire and work with someone who really knows the area well. With weaknesses, you can either learn enough to fix the issue, or you can hire someone to fix it. If you hire, you need to have enough understanding in the area to identify good help when they come along, and be a strong manager so you can both receive their help and attract their interest enough so they want to stay with you.

Personally, I do read in areas where I am strong, but I also travel with books in areas that I would prefer not to read. You won't grow by leisure reading. You have to purposefully select your intake.

Build a Well-Balanced Life

A well-balanced, successful, thriving life can be built. There is a road that leads there. Roads that lead to the mountain tops are not always well traveled, but the opportunity to get there is available to anyone who is willing to do it. This is a great time to review, take an inventory of your own life, and set out for the road that leads to the higher life.

First, get the foundation right. All life came from God. To live a full and deeply satisfied life, you need to live in harmony with the One who created it all. Are you spending time with God every day? Are you growing in your understanding of Him and the instructions He gave us for life? Are you living a life with a free conscience?

Second, make sure you have great relationships with people around you. If you are married, start with your marriage. Then look at your relationships with the rest of your immediate family. Continue on to friends and mentors. Do you have people in your life that are helping you grow? Are there others that you are helping to grow? And are you managing well those difficult relationships, making sure you are not carrying any grudges against anyone else?

Third, are you truly generous? Meaning, are you always looking to add to other people's lives? Or do you still prefer for others to be the ones that give to you? The happiest people are those who have learned to enjoy giving to others. Businesses that thrive are those that are adding value to all of their customers.

Fourth, are you continuously growing? Are you more valuable to others this year than you were last year? Are your daily habits better this year than they were last year? Are you constantly reading books or listening to podcasts that make you better?

Fifth, how are you doing with a system of dreaming, setting goals, and always working towards reaching those goals? Are you daily executing tasks that help you get where you want to go?

Sixth, are you proficient in all the basic areas? How are you doing in the handling of your personal finances? Do you have the right balance of giving, saving, and investing, or is too much going towards spending? If you are employed, do you know enough about your industry that other people on your job are asking you for advice? If you are in business, are you handling well all the basic areas of sales, marketing, management, and finance in addition to the operations of providing products or services to your customers?

Finally, are you balancing all the areas of life? Is there enough rest and enough fun activities? Remember, life is a journey. While it is good to set goals and work on designing our future, don't forget to enjoy the process. Find something to enjoy each and every day.

But now that you know how to get going, make sure you do something about it. The habit of learning, growing, and doing is too rewarding to live the alternative. There is a fork in the road and we each have a choice on what path we take.

Ignorance is expensive. Knowledge is cheap. Real wisdom is found in doing.

Epilogue

Wisdom for Meditation

... on his law he meditates day and night ...
In all that he does, he prospers.

-Psalm 1:2–3

Whenever there is an area of my life where I need to grow, an area I need strength, or an area I don't have clarity, I know that whatever God said in His Word is *the* truth in those areas.

I have made it a habit of searching the Bible and making myself a list of verses. I write them out and read the list daily, and meditate on those scriptures. The results are marvelous. Bit by bit, I build the truth into my life, and, bit by bit, my subconscious thinking changes and aligns itself to the truth. The results are that I start thinking, speaking, and acting in line with God's Word, and then start walking in victory in the area I had challenges. I have done this with healing, finances, relationships, peace, and several other areas. You can and should make your own lists and put this into practice immediately.

In sports, athletes practice the same moves over and over again. They practice the same steps for hours in order to build muscle memory. A basketball player practices ball handling so much, they don't have to think about how to handle the ball during a game. When the pressure of the game is on, their mind is on strategy, while their ball handling is automatic.

Meditation builds this kind of muscle memory in the mind. When you think on and mull over the truth of God's Word, it gets built into you so that when the pressures and temptations of life try to take control of you, it will still be God's Word that guides you.

The following is a sample to help get you started. These verses are arranged by topic. Take one of these topics and carefully read the scriptures every day for several days or weeks. Don't fall into the trap of browsing or quickly reading through these scriptures. That won't help you. God's Word is medicine, and medicine needs to be taken according to instructions. God's Word needs to be meditated on. Really focus on what you read in these verses. When you meditate on the scriptures, you build these truths into your subconsciousness. Over time, they will make a tremendous difference in your life, just like they have in mine.

Solomon on Success and Finances

A collection of scriptures from the book of Proverbs. I have placed a comment ahead of the scripture to help organize the list or to help bring out a point. Much of the content of this book came from meditating on this very list of verses.

IT ALL STARTS WITH REVERENCE OF GOD

Proverbs 1:7
The fear of the Lord is the beginning of knowledge;
fools despise wisdom and instruction.

THE LORD GIVES WISDOM

Proverbs 2:6
For the Lord gives wisdom;
from his mouth come knowledge and understanding

MAKE GOD FIRST PRIORITY

Proverbs 3:6–10
In all your ways acknowledge him,
and he will make straight your paths.

Be not wise in your own eyes;
fear the Lord, and turn away from evil.

It will be healing to your flesh
and refreshment to your bones.

Honor the Lord with your wealth
and with the firstfruits of all your produce;

then your barns will be filled with plenty,
and your vats will be bursting with wine.

WISDOM IS BETTER THAN MONEY

Proverbs 3:13–18
Blessed is the one who finds wisdom,
and the one who gets understanding,

for the gain from her is better than gain from silver
and her profit better than gold.

She is more precious than jewels,
and nothing you desire can compare with her.

Long life is in her right hand;
in her left hand are riches and honor.

Her ways are ways of pleasantness,
and all her paths are peace.

She is a tree of life to those who lay hold of her;
those who hold her fast are called blessed.

Proverbs 8:10–11
Take my instruction instead of silver,
and knowledge rather than choice gold,

for wisdom is better than jewels,
and all that you may desire cannot compare with her.

GUARD THE RELATIONSHIP WITH YOUR SPOUSE

Proverbs 5:3–5, 18–20, 23

For the lips of a forbidden woman drip honey,
and her speech is smoother than oil,

but in the end she is bitter as wormwood,
sharp as a two-edged sword.

Her feet go down to death;
her steps follow the path to Sheol; . . .

Let your fountain be blessed,
and rejoice in the wife of your youth,
a lovely deer, a graceful doe.

Let her breasts fill you at all times with delight;
be intoxicated always in her love.

Why should you be intoxicated, my son, with a forbidden
woman
and embrace the bosom of an adulteress? . . .

He dies for lack of discipline,
and because of his great folly he is led astray.

Proverbs 6:32–33

He who commits adultery lacks sense;
he who does it destroys himself.

He will get wounds and dishonor,
and his disgrace will not be wiped away.

SELF DISCIPLINE

Proverbs 6:6–11
Go to the ant, O sluggard;
consider her ways, and be wise.

Without having any chief,
officer, or ruler,

she prepares her bread in summer
and gathers her food in harvest.

How long will you lie there, O sluggard?
When will you arise from your sleep?

A little sleep, a little slumber,
a little folding of the hands to rest,

and poverty will come upon you like a robber,
and want like an armed man.

DO NOT ASSOCIATE WITH SINNERS

Proverbs 1:10, 15, 19
My son, if sinners entice you,
do not consent. . .

my son, do not walk in the way with them;
hold back your foot from their paths, . . .

Such are the ways of everyone who is greedy for unjust gain;
it takes away the life of its possessors.

CHOOSE HIGH MORALS

Proverbs 8:13
The fear of the Lord is hatred of evil.

Pride and arrogance and the way of evil
and perverted speech I hate.

ON THE PRIORITIES OF RICHES

Proverbs 3:13–15
Blessed is the one who finds wisdom,
and the one who gets understanding,

for the gain from her is better than gain from silver
and her profit better than gold.

She is more precious than jewels,
and nothing you desire can compare with her.

Proverbs 8:10–19
Take my instruction instead of silver,
and knowledge rather than choice gold,

for wisdom is better than jewels,
and all that you may desire cannot compare with her.

"I, wisdom, dwell with prudence,
and I find knowledge and discretion.

The fear of the Lord is hatred of evil.

Pride and arrogance and the way of evil
and perverted speech I hate.

I have counsel and sound wisdom;
I have insight; I have strength.

A FORK IN THE ROAD

By me kings reign,
and rulers decree what is just;

by me princes rule,
and nobles, all who govern justly.

I love those who love me,
and those who seek me diligently find me.

Riches and honor are with me,
enduring wealth and righteousness.

My fruit is better than gold, even fine gold,
and my yield than choice silver.

Proverbs 31:10
An excellent wife who can find?
She is far more precious than jewels.

ON RICHES GAINED HASTILY

Proverbs 13:11
Wealth gained hastily will dwindle,
but whoever gathers little by little will increase it.

Proverbs 21:5
The plans of the diligent lead surely to abundance,
but everyone who is hasty comes only to poverty.

Proverbs 28:22
A stingy man hastens after wealth
and does not know that poverty will come upon him.

ON BUSINESS ETHICS

Proverbs 11:1
A false balance is an abomination to the Lord,
but a just weight is his delight.

Proverbs 16:11
A just balance and scales are the Lord's;
all the weights in the bag are his work.

ON HUMILITY

Proverbs 13:18
Poverty and disgrace come to him who ignores instruction,
but whoever heeds reproof is honored..

Proverbs 15:33
The fear of the Lord is instruction in wisdom,
and humility comes before honor.

Proverbs 18:12
Before destruction a man's heart is haughty,
but humility comes before honor.

ON BEING LAZY AND WORKING DILIGENTLY OR HARD

Proverbs 6:10–11
A little sleep, a little slumber,
a little folding of the hands to rest,

and poverty will come upon you like a robber,
and want like an armed man.

Proverbs 10:4
A slack hand causes poverty,
but the hand of the diligent makes rich.

Proverbs 12:11
Whoever works his land will have plenty of bread,
but he who follows worthless pursuits lacks sense.

Proverbs 12:24
The hand of the diligent will rule,
while the slothful will be put to forced labor.

Proverbs 20:4
The sluggard does not plow in the autumn;
he will seek at harvest and have nothing.

Proverbs 20:13
Love not sleep, lest you come to poverty;
open your eyes, and you will have plenty of bread.

Proverbs 21:5
The plans of the diligent lead surely to abundance,
but everyone who is hasty comes only to poverty.

Proverbs 24:30—34
I passed by the field of a sluggard,
by the vineyard of a man lacking sense,

and behold, it was all overgrown with thorns;
the ground was covered with nettles,
and its stone wall was broken down.

Then I saw and considered it;
I looked and received instruction.

A little sleep, a little slumber,
a little folding of the hands to rest,

and poverty will come upon you like a robber,
and want like an armed man.

Proverbs 28:19
Whoever works his land will have plenty of bread,
but he who follows worthless pursuits will have plenty
of poverty.

Proverbs 31:13
She seeks wool and flax,
and works with willing hands.

ON LOVING PLEASURE OR THE GOOD LIFE

Proverbs 21:17
Whoever loves pleasure will be a poor man;
he who loves wine and oil will not be rich.

ON GENEROSITY TOWARDS THE POOR

Proverbs 17:5
Whoever mocks the poor insults his Maker;
he who is glad at calamity will not go unpunished.

Proverbs 19:17
Whoever is generous to the poor lends to the Lord,
and he will repay him for his deed.

Proverbs 21:13
Whoever closes his ear to the cry of the poor
will himself call out and not be answered.

Proverbs 22:16
Whoever oppresses the poor to increase his own wealth,
or gives to the rich, will only come to poverty.

Proverbs 28:27
Whoever gives to the poor will not want,
but he who hides his eyes will get many a curse.

Proverbs 31:20
She opens her hand to the poor
and reaches out her hands to the needy.

ON GENEROSITY

Proverbs 3:9
Honor the Lord with your wealth
and with the firstfruits of all your produce.

Proverbs 11:24–26

One gives freely, yet grows all the richer;
another withholds what he should give, and only suffers
want.

Whoever brings blessing will be enriched,
and one who waters will himself be watered.

The people curse him who holds back grain,
but a blessing is on the head of him who sells it.

Proverbs 18:16

A man's gift makes room for him
and brings him before the great.

Proverbs 22:9

Whoever has a bountiful eye will be blessed,
for he shares his bread with the poor.

ON STRIVING TO GET RICH

Proverbs 23:4

Do not toil to acquire wealth;
be discerning enough to desist.

ON GREED AND BEING CONTENT

Proverbs 30:8–9
Remove far from me falsehood and lying;
give me neither poverty nor riches;
feed me with the food that is needful for me,

lest I be full and deny you
and say, "Who is the Lord?"

or lest I be poor and steal
and profane the name of my God.

Proverbs 28:25
A greedy man stirs up strife,
but the one who trusts in the Lord will be enriched.

Proverbs 28:8
Whoever multiplies his wealth by interest and profit
gathers it for him who is generous to the poor.

TRUSTING IN RICHES OR TRUSTING IN GOD

Proverbs 11:12
Whoever belittles his neighbor lacks sense,
but a man of understanding remains silent.

Further Resources

I have included a list of resources to help you grow in various areas. I would encourage you to find the areas in your life where you would like to grow further, then read books, listen to podcasts, and listen to people who have experience in that area.

God Wants You Prosperous

Thou Shall Prosper: Ten Commandments for Making Money by Daniel Lapin

Create Your Future

Think and Grow Rich by Napoleon Hill

The Richest Man Who Ever Lived by Steven K. Scott

The Magic of Thinking Big by David J. Schwartz

Kick the Dependency Syndrome

How Should We Then Live?: The Rise and Decline of Western Thought and Culture by Francis Schaffer

Becoming Gold

Signposts on the Road to Success by E.W. Kenyon

What About the Money?

The Blessed Life by Robert Morris

How to Receive God's Extravagant Generosity by Mark Hankins

The Midas Touch by Kenneth E. Hagin

Rich Dad, Poor Dad by Robert Kiyosaki

Increase Your Financial IQ by Robert Kiyosaki

Financial Peace by Dave Ramsey

The Total Money Makeover by Dave Ramsey

Dreams and Visions

The 7 Habits of Highly Effective People: Powerful Lessons in Personal Change by Stephen R. Covey

The Art of Getting Things Done by Clay Clark

Eat That Frog!: 21 Great Ways to Stop Procrastinating and Get More Done in Less Time by Brian Tracy

Walking With God

Listen to Your Heart by Kenneth W. Hagin

How to Read the Bible for All Its Worth by Gordon D. Fee & Douglas Stuart

How to Study the Word by Terry Lawson

Building Bridges

Marriage on the Rock by Jimmy Evans

Love & Respect by Emerson Eggerichs

The Peacemaker by Ken Sande

Be a People Person by John Maxwell

How to Win Friends & Influence People by Dale Carnegie

Love: The Way to Victory by Kenneth E. Hagin

The Five Love Languages by Gary Chapman

The Greatest Thing in the World by Henry Drummond

Continual Growth

Your Best Life Now by Joel Osteen

The Rhythm of Life by Richard Exley

About Safari Mission

Safari Mission is a nonprofit mission organization based in Tulsa, OK. Vidar and Cathrine Ligard are the founders and executive directors of SafariMission.org. They work on reversing the dependency syndrome that plagues Africa and teach

people to come out of poverty and fix their broken systems. Many lives and communities have been changed through the work, and the people continue to teach other people in their communi-  ties the same principles. The organization has a strong emphasis on ethics and leadership. Safari Mission focuses on giving people the knowledge and tools they need to build their own lives and the community around them. These are long-term methods that solve the real problem instead of band-aid fixes. Please visit **www.safarimission.org** for more information and testimonials.

Become a Supporter

Are you able to give $5 a month to train leaders in East Africa? For the price of a cup of coffee, you can be a part of making lasting change in people's lives. For every 65 people who give $5 a month, Safari Mission is able to train up to 40 leaders in rural East Africa. Become a partner and help people change their lives, families, and communities today.

**Go to <u>www.safarimission.org/donate</u>
or text the amount to 918-994-1999.**

Finding Jesus

Prosperity is great. Having the means to not only take care of yourself and your family, but to be a blessing to others as well is an amazing feeling. But none of that matters if you don't have peace within yourself and peace with God. And the only way to have that peace is by having a relationship with the Prince of Peace—Jesus. And He died on the cross for you, your sins, and so you can have peace with God. If you have never asked Jesus to be your Lord and Savior or maybe you need to rededicate your life to Him, simply pray the following prayer:

Dear God, I come to You right now in the name of Jesus. I know that I am a sinner, and I confess my sins to You. I confess with my mouth that Jesus is Lord, and I believe in my heart that You raised Him from the dead. Because of that, I thank You that I am saved, and I have peace with You.

In Jesus name I pray,

Amen.

If you prayed this prayer, I would love to hear from you. You can reach me at office@safarimission.org

CPSIA information can be obtained
at www.ICGtesting.com
Printed in the USA
JSHW040232270621
16216JS00002B/12